Five Weeks: a Lifetime

The True Journey of Clinton Jacob

Hannah Sullivan

This book is dedicated to our baby boy, Clinton Jacob Sullivan: In memory and in strength. To those who helped, loved, rejoiced, and mourned: You carry his light. To my own family: May we live in love and grow in peace.

CONTENTS

A Note from the Author

YOU HOLD IN YOUR HANDS the beating of my heart, a tempo that brings joy to my soul and thrums its rhythm throughout my daily life. Originally meant as a journal to pass on to my third child when he was grown, I offer it now to you. Within these pages lives the story of Clinton, a boy of strength and courage, told through journal entries, emails, conversations, and letters. It is a very true measure of our life, and I welcome you to enter and stay awhile.

If you have further thoughts, questions, ideas, or your own story to share, please feel free to contact me at Thunderstorybooks@gmail.com or look me up on my website at http://www.thunderstories.com/

With much love, Hannah

From the Beginning

Learning I was pregnant was an exciting, fresh start for our family. This would be our third child, much anticipated, and very much loved—even before the pink "plus" showed on the test stick.

Our joy at the news was even sweeter, due to the sadness we'd felt four months prior, when we'd had an early miscarriage. Our first doctor's appointment for that pregnancy had been scheduled for a Monday; instead, the Thursday before, I called my sister.

"Something's not right, Sarah." My voice waivered and I felt the phone shake in my grip. "I'm spotting and haven't felt really nauseous for a few days."

"Oh, Hannie. What are you going to do?"

"I don't know; I mean, it is what it is. If something is wrong ..." I couldn't even voice the "M" word, "... there's nothing I can do to change anything. We just have to wait and see."

That night my husband, John, called his friend, Mike, whose wife was a nurse on the maternity ward at a hospital in California. He hung up and somberly stated, "Hannah, Amy says spotting early in the pregnancy isn't a sure sign of anything, but we should call the doctor if it turns heavy or any clots come out."

On Friday, John came home early from work and called the doctor. I told our daughter, who was a little over two and a half but wise beyond her years, that her baby wasn't ready to come yet; it would join us when it was. Our prenatal appointment on Monday became a check-up to verify that my body was healthy. And empty.

So, the news at the end of March 2006, that a baby was again trying to join our family came as a happy thrill. I purchased a baby journal as soon as possible. I wanted to record everything.

*****

April

The Journal Begins

4-7-06

FOR AS LONG AS I CAN REMEMBER, I have wanted to be a mama. I've always loved children. Before Ellie and Mikey showed up, I took care of other people's kiddos. I knew one day I'd have my own. We started with Eleanor Rose, who was born on March 24, 2003, then Michael Joseph, born on December 8, 2004, and now you, due December 7, 2006. That's kind of cool, to have a birthday so close to your big brother's! We are so excited that you're on the way. I can't wait for our first prenatal check-up; you have no idea how long we've waited for you.

The reason I adore kids? Kids just see and express things so much better than grownups. Somehow honest and beautiful, even when faulty thinking comes into play! I went to school for early childhood education and worked as a toddler teacher and as a nanny for several years, until I was finally at a point where I could stop raising other people's kids and start raising my own!

~*~

THE LAST COUPLE OF MONTHS, I kept thinking I was pregnant, only to find out I wasn't. This month, I felt completely not pregnant. We were right at the end of preparing for our move from Idaho to Montana, so we'd been pretty busy, but I was still very aware of the date and the fact that something hadn't happened yet. I didn't want to take a test too early and get a false answer so I waited until I was pretty sure I had to be pregnant.

When we sold our house in Idaho, we stayed in a hotel for two nights before your dad—Poppy—began his drive in one of the moving trucks to Kalispell, Montana. Poppy used to be just "Pop," until one day when Ellie got a bad owie. She bellowed, "Poppy! Popppyyy!" like she needed the mommy part of her Pop to come fix it. The name stuck. Any-hoo, Ellie, Mikey, and I stayed at our next-door neighbor's for two more nights before flying out to join Poppy. On March 31—just a week ago!—the first morning in our hotel room, I took THE test and sure enough, you're on the way!

We are so happy. Ellie was the first to know, as she was with me when I took the test—never do you have privacy as a parent! I gave her the stick and told her to bring it to Poppy. Then I told Poppy that Ellie had something to show him.

Taking the stick, he saw the bright "+" sign. "Are you really?!" A big goofy grin spread over his face; and then we told Mikey, who said "Yeah!"—his favorite word at sixteen months.

Ellie was adamant: "It's a baby bruver."

We went to the hotel lobby for breakfast, acting as if we were not on the cusp of a brand new life. All proper and sedate, except for our random giggles and shining eyes. I could have tap-danced on the table! Before Poppy had to leave, we called a few people to share the news; they all knew how much we wanted another baby and responded with happiness at our words.

When I talked to Aunt Sarah, she was excited for us. She shrieked into the phone and I'm pretty sure she was jumping up and down. Poppy's dad, Grandpa Mike (who will be moving from Hawaii to Montana in a month), told Poppy, "That's great—another reason to get over there as soon as I can."

Poppy's brother, Uncle Jeff, came down from Kalispell to help Poppy drive the moving truck. He met us in the hotel parking lot. We probably looked slightly demented with our grins. Poppy said,

"So, are you ready to help the five of us move?" A quick pause and then a return grin—with us currently being a family of four, it didn't take Jeff long to do the math.

Later, we told Miss Kim (a friend in Idaho), who was thrilled, and my brother, Uncle Seth, who said his typical "That's cool." Grandmas Nana and Betsy were both excited when they heard, and Grandpa Miles echoed your other grandpa with a "That's great."

We have now told friends, relatives, and, yes, strangers, who are all so happy to hear our news! No waiting around for us; we want to spread our happiness! Thinking about you makes me feel warm and sparkly.

4-10-06

TODAY, I AM DREAMING about when you're going to be born …. I was born in the middle of summer on July 12, 1978, at home, by your Grandma Nana's choice. She had me in a bedroom on the second floor of our un-air-conditioned house—the first floor was actually a toy store called The Ark. That day, Grandma saw a dead, coiled snake on the stairs.

A midwife and my dad helped deliver me while my sister Sarah (four years old) and brother Seth (two years old) were at a friend's house. I was small—less than six pounds—and it was extremely hot. I ended up going to the hospital anyway when I was a couple days old, due to dehydration. My parents were both thirty years old (for comparison, I'll be twenty-eight with you). Grandma was a stay-at home mom (like me) and I believe grandpa was teaching at the time; he became a nurse several years later. Oh! I was born in Fair Oaks, California, near Sacramento. I lived in pretty much the same area until Poppy and I moved out of state to Idaho, when Ellie was eight months old.

Poppy—John—was born on January 4, 1974, weighing nine pounds and fifteen ounces. His parents were twenty-five years old. He was their second, and last, child. Born in Indio, California, near

Palm Springs, the amazing thing weather-wise about his birth was that it snowed in the desert, closing parts of the freeway!

Speaking of Poppy, he and I met at work—a pharmacy called Longs Drugs—where I was an ancillary, or a counter girl, and he was the weekend pharmacist. I think we both liked each other from the get-go and soon everybody else knew, too. They even tried to get us scheduled together on the same weekends! On our first date, he picked me up at work and we walked down the sidewalk to an Italian restaurant. We dated for a few years, moved around a bunch, and got married on March 10, 2002 in Sacramento, California.

I hope you inherit Poppy's strength, calmness, and levelheadedness. He's great if there's ever a crisis! Also, it would be grand if you shared his sense of dedication and of right and wrong, the like of hands-on work, and of carrying through until the task is complete.

I hope you enjoy reading or sports and exercise or drawing like I do (or find your own substitutes for those, which fit your personality). And I hope you are open-minded, loving, and into family.

Being kind of a surprise, you make me thankful I don't have any bad habits that will/would be harmful to you. I don't drink alcohol and think smoking is icky and dangerous (yeah, I know: total mom mode!). I don't take medications either, and I'm a pretty healthy person. I take my prenatal vitamin every night and try to walk or run a few miles at least five days a week. I probably like sweets—especially chocolate—too much for my own good, but I don't binge on it or anything! I've just started feeling nauseated within the last couple of days, so food of any kind is just NOT sounding good. I'm trying to eat as healthfully as I can for us.

~*~

GUESS WHAT I JUST FIGURED OUT? We're starting off in spring … a time of newness, growth, and hope. And how appropriate! Not only do we have a new little one on the way, but we've got a new town, state, house, job, everything!

My favorite seasons are fall and winter. I love cold blustery days, loud storms, and snowfall—mainly so I can be all snuggled up in the inside warmth. Also, I love the fall colors of the trees, the smell of smoke in the air, the birds honking and calling as they fly away, and, of course, I adore all the holidays and yummy treats to go with them!

I'll be keeping some of my journal slots open, in case I think of something more to write on a topic. Who knows? I may come up with brilliant thoughts to add. And, in case you're wondering why there are fifty gazillion entries for a particular day, well your sister and brother are young and I just grab snippets of time to write. Each time I return to it, and especially if it's a new topic, I slap on the date and plow ahead.

~*~

MY FAMILY (ELLIE, MIKEY, POPPY, AND NOW YOU) are the most prized things in my life. Not meaning that you're possessions at all! Anything could happen to anything I own, and life would go on. But I don't know how I'd pull through if anything were to happen to any of you.

~*~

SO FAR, I have no cravings or aversions; food in general just DOES NOT sound good!

4-21-06

I AM SO EXCITED! I can't tell you how long I've been waiting for you! You are such a special part of our family already. Ellie talks about you daily. Within the last four to five days, my belly has ballooned! I get all mushy just thinking about you growing in there. I can't believe we're under two months and you're showing SO MUCH. I can't wait for you to move around in there!

~*~

YOUR POPPY IS A SUPER PERSON, a great man, and a loving father and husband. He is dedicated to "doing what's right, because it's the right thing to do," even if it's the harder way to go, and I totally respect him for that. As a protector and provider, he is a trustworthy person who we can all look up to. He loves golf, coffee, camping, and woodworking (really, doing anything that uses tools). He is patient and playful—great for you kids. At six feet and three inches, he is tall, with red-brown hair and hazel eyes. Although he's a pharmacist, he'd prefer to be a pro-golfer!

Me? I believe in "all things for a reason," but you also have to own your choices and decisions. I like things to be "nice and tidy"—whether it's a room or an emotion! I think I need more patience; other than that, I'm pretty even tempered. I'm smallish, around 5 feet 2 inches with medium length light brown hair and hazel eyes. My favorite things to do for myself are drawing, painting, reading, and running. My favorite things in general? Lounging outside, listening to the birds, and watching the kids play together.

~*~

WELL! With you, Little One, I have been quite nauseated and blah (just not for the first week I knew about you) and have thrown up several times, but (and you'll probably think I'm crazy), I'm loving it. I love being pregnant and knowing you're on your way. Feeling sick is reassuring to me that you're okay and growing well. If I don't take a nap, I get pretty tired, but I can still function. Every day I try to run a couple miles, which makes me feel healthier.

As long as I keep sipping water, my tummy seems to stay out of the puking thing, which is good. So far, there has been no trick food that gets me through … NOTHING sounds good and, besides water, there's no guarantee that my tummy will settle down!

May

5-3-06

BESIDES THE KIDS AND POPPY, we have one dog, named Shilah, which we got a couple of years before Ellie showed up. We also had some fish before we moved. That's it for pets!

~*~

ALL MY BABY BOOKS ARE STILL IN STORAGE; it's driving me bonkers because I want to be reading about your progress! Also, I've been feeling a little plip and pop every once in a while. I'm wondering if it's you, but it seems early?!

~*~

I'M NOT BIG ON SHOPPING, spending money, hanging out in stores, etc. Pretty much the only things I buy for myself are books—I have tons. Every once in a while, I'll get a DVD movie or some Jelly Bellies, but not too often. I also like to buy toys for you kids—things that I think you'd have fun with and learn from at the same time! Poppy and I sometimes go out on dinner and movie dates; I really enjoy that, too!

~*~

POPPY IS A TOTAL TRUCK GUY. I have a Ford Expedition, a big SUV that can hold eight people. I really like it, but the newer model is even better and one day I'd like to upgrade! I got this car because tall

Poppy and short Mommy can easily fit in it, as well as all the children that we care to have!

~*~

I AM THE THIRD CHILD in a family of four (Sarah, Seth, me, and then Grace). My favorite memories of growing up are the feelings of magic and surprises around every corner. We believed in fairies, elves, and angels (still do!). Sarah—four years older than me— helped create houses for the Littles to find; we even stocked them with supplies like lace-leaves for blankets and plant parts for dishes and furniture. If any of us left a blank piece of paper inside by the front door, during the night it would be filled with pictures and notes from the fairies.

Holidays, especially Christmas, were magical—gleaming with silver and gold, lit candles, a crackling fire, treats, songs, togetherness—a feeling of warmth and love. (Probably why I love winter so much.) I also remember building block towns with Seth and reading stories with Sarah. I loved when Grace, who is seven years younger than I am, would fall asleep on me.

~*~

THIS PAST MONTH HAS BEEN CRAZY! For most of it, we've all been sick. We've been living with Uncle Jeff and Aunt Cindi for that time, too, since our house still isn't finished. Our builder is hit and miss, and Poppy is working long hours at the hospital and isn't actually, um, a house builder.

It was busy with so many people inside one house. (They, too, are expecting a baby and have one little daughter, Nina, and a dog named Wheezer.) Let me tell you, mommy was at her limit some days, but we got by. It was amazing of Jeff and Cindi to welcome all of us into their home for that length of time; they didn't have to do that! Your big brother and sister did really well. Having them around and knowing that you're coming kept me focused and moving forward. Running also helped, just getting outside and gulping in the fresh air.

Thankfully, we just moved into Grandpa Mike's empty house two days ago. We get to housesit and have our own space until our house is completed. This part of Montana is gorgeous; I love it.

~*~

PEOPLE LIKE ASKING ABOUT the age spacing between you kids or my take on when a person should become a parent. They usually assume I'm really young. It makes me laugh. I was twenty-three when we got married, twenty-four when we had Ellie. My take is you "should" become a parent if and when you're ready for it! Could be when you're twenty or when you're forty. I don't think age really matters if you are mature enough and have enough love within you.

The main thing I've observed as a childcare teacher, nanny, and mom, is that, as a parent, you need to raise your family in a way that is right for you, your spouse, and your children. Not what's right for anyone else—regardless of what peers, mothers, mothers-in-law, strangers, or the media may say.

Listen to the doctors, read the books, get tips from those around you whom you respect. Choose the information that works for your ideals and ethics. Go with it, adapt it, and strive to do your best. As long as it's done with love, don't second-guess yourself (at least not in front of the kids). Never do anything that will harm them (or you) physically, emotionally, or mentally. The whole point of being a parent is leading a child on a lifelong journey, showing a way for him/her to reach his/her best and fullest potential as a functioning adult. Also consistency, follow-through, and scheduling (based on the child's needs) are KEY!

~*~

YOU'LL BE BORN at Poppy's hospital, Kalispell Regional Medical Center (KRMC). I'm most comfortable with that kind of delivery. Grandma Nana had me at home, but my siblings were all born in hospitals. Given the era, she probably stayed in the hospital longer than I did with your brother and sister (which is twenty-four hours or under). I don't know if she took any medications for her deliveries, but I went all natural with your siblings and plan to do the same with you. Grandpa Miles was at our births, just as Poppy was for Ellie and Mikey and will be for you.

Growing up, I remember both of my parents being hands-on and involved, understanding the magic of childhood ... giving us rules

11

and chores while giving us room to make our choices and explore our environment and ourselves. We helped in the garden and with taking care of ducks, chickens, and rabbits. We picked fruit from our trees to sell for spending money. We took family walks, had sit-down meals, family story time before bed, special traditions, etc. These are some of the things I try to carry over to your lives!

~*~

I BELIEVE THAT pretty much everyone we meet, no matter how small or insignificant that meeting may seem to be, has an impact on who we are and on how we live our lives. Take one person, one factor, out of your past, and you may make a different choice that leads you down a different path.

~*~

RIGHT AT THE BEGINNING of the second month, my belly began to bulge out! It looks so big to me, and we've not even completed two months yet! Twins? I've been wearing the clothes I wore with Ellie and Mikey, but it's time I found something new. Maternity clothes now are nice. Almost any clothing store carries them, and you can be as up-to-date or fuddy-duddy as you want! And as casual or dressy, too! At the moment, I fall under "fuddy-duddy"—I think I need to give in and shop.

5-9-06

I AM SO THANKFUL for our family. Poppy, Ellie, and Mikey are all amazing and wonderful people. They add so much to my life— love, laughter, happiness, friendship—and now, with you on the way, I am all the more thankful for the love we have in our family. How lucky am I to have you growing within me?!

I am also thankful to live where we do. It's a gorgeous area without too many (or too few) people.

I'm thankful I get to be at home and raise you kids and that Poppy is able to do the work he does and can support us. I am thankful that we are all healthy, smart, and rational. ;-)

~*~

TO GO ALONG WITH my being fuddy-duddy, you might as well add "old!" Compared to my own growing-up years, yours will be much different. You'll be part of a generation with cell phones, TVs attached to everything, and new ways of listening to music (iPods, internet radio, satellite radio, etc.). You'll have access to cars that start with the push of a button (or open doors at the push of a button), internet, huge TVs that look like you're looking through a window as the picture is so pristine, any kind of plastic toy you can imagine, all sorts of gadgets for computers, games, etc.

I come from a generation where car air-conditioning was sometimes just the window rolled down; bicycle seats were shaped like a long, yellow fruit; socks were worn in layers over pegged pants; and the remote was actually connected to the VCR. Which was rented. And was a VCR. Will you even know what the term "rewind" means?

~*~

KALISPELL REGIONAL MEDICAL CENTER is about twenty-five to thirty minutes away (depending on the time, weather, and if I am the one driving). We'll take the straightest route to get us there when it's time. My first two labors were way quick, and we'd like to have you born in the hospital, not on the side of the road! Ellie and Mikey will stay with Grandpa Mike, who will come over to be with them when we're ready.

5-21-06

I'M PRETTY SURE I have been feeling you move around a little bit. There will be a slight pressure and then one little plip against my belly. My hand even moved out with one. I can't find my books in storage, so I can't look up when it's typical to start feeling movement! We're still in the middle of our incredibly long three month move and hope to goodness our house will be done soon!

~*~

CHOCOLATE SOUNDS SOOO GOOD, but I don't usually keep much around. (I'd eat it all!) I need to keep drinking water in order not to get sick. Making meals is a hard task—smells and textures really get me icky. I'm the main cook, too. I think I cook pretty well, though not too creatively. The kids really love pastas (so did I before you!). I make a mean garlic mashed potato, but I can't stomach garlic right now. Most of my meals are quick and easy. I think they taste good and lean towards the healthier side (though I know we could lean in that direction even more). Since you, I've been making lots of pastas to please the kids, as I know I won't be eating much anyway.

~*~

WHAT CAN I TELL YOU about the news and popular fads, so you can look back at this journal and laugh? Hmm: not much! I don't really keep tabs on what's happening in the news. It always seems so glum and dreadful, so I guess you wouldn't laugh at that anyway. I know there's still a war going on in, sheesh, I think it's Iraq. A lot of people think we should pull our troops out. I don't know.

Fashion? Seems like anything goes, which works for me. I've always been a jeans and tee-shirt gal. Silly diets seem to have tapered out (some were so popular just a year ago, but I think all that stuff is unhealthy). It's starting to take the better route of healthy eating and exercise.

June

6-8-06

Our first doctor's appointment was today. I'm fourteen weeks and one day pregnant! Holy smokes, I already weigh in at 131 pounds! That's so incredibly high for me, but, honestly, I'm not going to worry about it. I feel so very fit and healthy. We go for a three-mile run about five to seven days a week. I usually eat pretty well, though you've been giving me some pretty sweet cravings—junky ones, too—like cheese puffs. I never eat that kind of stuff but so little sounds good, I've been eating what I can!

The appointment was good; the nurses and nurse practitioner were really nice. We just filled out paperwork and covered past health info, previous pregnancies, and current concerns—I've become dizzy and lightheaded a couple of times, to the point where my vision goes black. They drew blood (which already has become a two-inch bruise) and such. The best, most special part was that we got to hear your heartbeat! Oh, it was amazing! And, oh, Honey, you are so real!

Poppy, Ellie, and Mikey were with me, which made it a special moment for all of us. Ellie asked all sorts of questions, talked about ultrasounds, and smiled hugely at the galloping sound of your heart (she's three years and two months old). Mikey got really still in

Poppy's arms and listened (he's eighteen months old today). Poppy and I grinned from ear to ear. There's something completely magical about hearing your tiny heartbeat pumping away inside your body inside my body. Amazing. Of course, with a growing belly, you are a visible physical part of me/us, but hearing you makes you seem so much more … I don't know … alive and real, I guess.

6-9-06

I HAVE A GROUP OF DOCTORS and any one of them can end up delivering you. I haven't met any of them yet (just the nurse practitioner, who is very nice), but they're supposed to be really good—the sought after doctors of the area! I chose them for that reason and for the fact that they're at the hospital where you will be delivered. Our insurance is pretty good and covers most everything, except the initial fee. Still kind of nervous about the office and hospital being so far from us, since you're due during a Montana winter.

~*~

ULTRASOUND!!!! Oh my gosh, we had our first ultrasound and guess what?! We're really sixteen weeks along today and your due date is November 24, 2006, not December 7! So neat that you're coming sooner than expected! It was amazing to see you on the screen.

You already look like a "real" baby, and we were expecting a little bean shape. We saw your head, the curve of your back, your little rump, and even your feet! Golly, it was so neat. Ellie asked all sorts of questions about the instruments, goop, you, etc., while Mikey was most interested in the room-divider curtains! He grew still and paid attention, though, as the technician listened to your heartbeat. You are beautiful and I can't wait to hold and snuggle you.

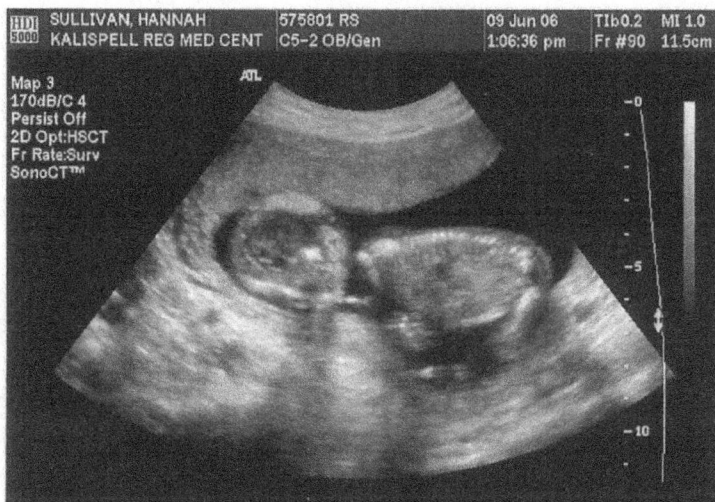

DEFINITELY A BABY AND NOT A BEAN. WE'RE FURTHER ALONG THAN EXPECTED.

~*~

I HAVEN'T FELT MUCH activity from you but, when I lie on my belly, I feel like I'm lying on top of something. I can't wait to hold you and breathe in your baby smell. Ahhh, nothing beats that scent!

~*~

WE'VE ALREADY CELEBRATED Easter with you as a baby bump. Now we'll have July 4th, Halloween, and Thanksgiving (maybe!). My favorite holiday of all time is Christmas—the whole Christmas season! It has always seemed so warm, magical, and shimmery. Full of love, food, and memories. An actual family experience. I really hope we can recreate that for you and your siblings.

Growing up, we celebrated Advent, St. Nicholas, Christmas, Three Kings Day, and even Hanukkah! (Grandpa Miles comes from a Jewish family.) You should be able to spend your first couple of weeks basking in that glow of love and joy and peace— all multiplied this year because of your arrival!

~*~

POPPY HAS RECENTLY become an unofficial builder and has been trying to finish our new house so we can finally move in! Our builder seems to have disappeared ....

~*~

POPPY AND I DON'T GET too much time together, where it's really just the two of us. When we do, we usually spend the time watching a movie or TV show, inventing our own games, playing cribbage, or just hanging out. We like looking at the lights of the town from our back patio.

~*~

POPPY IS A PHARMACIST. His father is one, too, and Poppy grew up helping in his dad's pharmacy. I think this is one reason he chose his profession. I think he likes being able to help people and likes learning new things. He is constantly learning in his work.

~*~

SO MUCH MAKES ME HAPPY! Knowing you're growing within me. Watching Ellie and Mikey playing together and loving each other. Seeing their love for Poppy and me. Watching Poppy be involved with the kids and doing work he enjoys. Reading a really good book. Going for a run and being able to see the beauty around me. Being warm and toasty in a magnificent thunderstorm. Watching snowflakes. Lying outside on a blanket with my eyes closed and hearing the chirping of birds and insects. Up-beat songs and movies … so much! My "prescription"? I figure, in life, there are so many times where you can either laugh or cry, and I would so much rather be able to laugh. Laughter seems much more productive.

I'm a sucker for positive thinking and believe strength and self-reliance should come from within. I like quotes, like: "You can't always get what you want, but you can want what you have," or "Do what you can with what you have," or the serenity prayer ("God, grant me the serenity to accept the things I cannot change, the courage to change the things I can, and the wisdom to know the difference."). Of course, those are probably mangled versions, but that's the gist of them. I also like "If you want it done right, do it yourself," "Do whatever you do to the best of your ability," and "There's no such thing as what might have been." I guess my favorite quotes are about self/independence/taking care of business on your own. All that stuff is important to me. Be your OWN self, stay true to that, and always try your best. (Otherwise, what's the point?)

~*~

WHILE I DON'T BELIEVE in superstitions, I do believe in signs, good luck, and "all things for a reason." I think we all have a purpose here on earth and that eventually we all fulfill it, no matter how many times we have to live to get it done right! (Yes, I believe in re-incarnation.) I think we learn from all the experiences in our lives, and that things come our way that we need to learn from.

~*~

SOME OF MY FAVORITES, so you know 'em. Favorite smells: sweet roses; blossoms; yummy food cooking; the earth after the rain; Poppy's shirts; soft, downy baby heads; a clean, open, and airy house … lots of things! My favorite smells to wear—which I don't do often—are fruity smells like peach, raspberry, or melon. Favorite colors: dusty shades of blues and greens (the lighter tones, not the jewel tones), cranberry/pomegranate reds, and rusty autumny oranges. Flowers: irises, violets, daffodils, day lilies, roses, bright colors! Sounds: water (rain, the ocean, rivers, etc.) and the wind through the leaves—which, I guess, can sound like water. ;-)

~*~

I'M EASY TO PLEASE. To me, the greatest treat is some time to myself with several good books, some yummy munchies, and a big soft bed. Throw us all together and I'm as happy as can be!!!

~*~

I PLAN TO NURSE you because it is the best and healthiest choice for you. (Plus, it's free!) It really bugs me when people say you need to nurse for bonding, that it's such a great way to bond, blah blah blah bond. I think there are so many ways— a lifetime—to bond with your child; snuggling, cuddling, and holding your child are excellent ways to do so, without requiring them to suck on a part of your body for a year or more! Yes, it's great, wonderful, and natural (and a way to bond, tee-hee), but don't look down on bottle-feeders. Parents who use bottles can bond just as well with their child. Besides, just because a baby's drinking from a bottle doesn't mean it's not drinking breast milk! Not that formula's bad, because it's not. Who are we to judge? There's bound to be a reason behind either choice. Anyway, nursing has always been easy for me. It's true: if it hurts, you're doing it wrong!

6-11-06

WE HAVE finally moved in!

6-18-06

I DON'T THINK THERE ARE an ideal number of years to space between children. I think it depends on the individual children and the family as a whole. I've known people who have bemoaned or praised the same amount of years between their kids. Close to twenty months has worked well with us. The kids are great friends, and they are VERY excited about you!

6-22-06

AT LAST! The final boxes are in the garage (well, we still have stuff in storage, but we need to finish the basement before we can move that.) The house is mostly put together and decorated (some furniture needs to be purchased still, too), but it looks good and is very livable.

~*~

NOW THAT YOU'RE ON THE WAY, I'm more in tune with families with lots of young kids and babies. They're everywhere! When I see little babies, it shocks me how small and vulnerable they are. You forget those things as your children grow. As a parent, to know you are responsible for the brand new life of this being, of its growth and safety and well-being? The responsibility is incredible; the magnitude and importance of the job are mind blowing. Here is a creature who relies on you for its very survival. Whew, boy!

~*~

I LOVE MORNINGS when it's cool and crisp and the world seems slow, and the kids and I can hear all the birds chirping on our runs. I love afternoons because we all nap, which is the best thing in the world. I love the evening and seeing the sunset. I love the in-between times when we can play, laugh, and have adventures. Right now, in the evenings, after the dinner stuff comes the bath stuff; then, Mikey goes to bed. Ellie and I cuddle and read or whatever; then, she goes to bed. Finally, I get ready for bed (sounds exciting!). Usually, I read or watch decorating shows (I don't watch TV during the day, really).

~*~

DEFINITE MOVEMENT! You are not a soft delicate "plipper"; you do quick firm jabs! I've been doing a ton of unpacking and moving of boxes and hanging of pictures and, for the past couple of days, I've felt something going on in your area. I haven't known if it was just me tweaking my body in a weird way (which has happened two times now, where I've twisted my body and my whole tummy makes a "pop" feeling and seems to shift over). Yesterday and several times today, you have moved while I was just sitting. Very exciting, surprising, and shocking because I was expecting plips, not full-on jabs! Oh, Honey, I can't wait to see you.

~*~

WITHIN THE LAST WEEK OR TWO, my tummy has been so much better. Food still doesn't sound good, but I still run around three miles a day. That feels good.

July

7-18-06

I HAD A DOCTOR'S APPOINTMENT TODAY, and I think we're twenty-one weeks along??? Welp, I actually had an appointment a week ago (and according to the chart, you're due November *20th*!). Then today we had your official ultrasound and a follow-up with the doctor. There are three in the group and they're all super people.

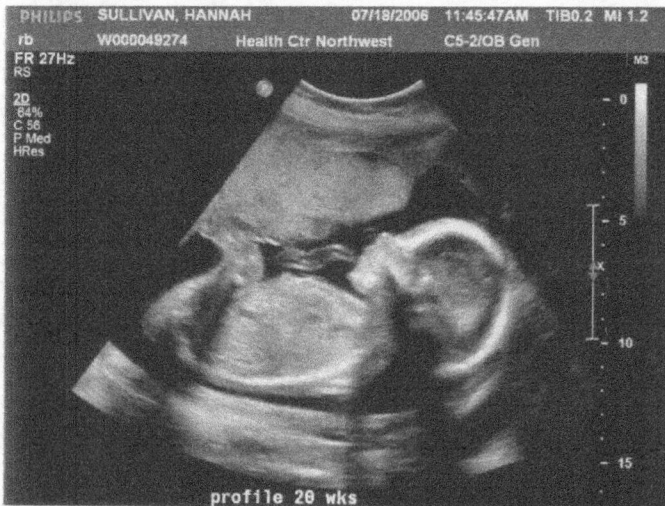

A BABY THIS AGE HAS A HEART THE SIZE OF A WALNUT.

It was so amazing seeing you on the screen—your little nose and feet are especially cute. Ellie was beyond excited to see you on the screen. We get to see a specialist when we return from Uncle Seth's wedding (next month) because you may need help with your heart. So, you'd better hold on tight in there and be strong! You're not supposed to make us worry before you're born! (Okay, don't make us worry after either!) The appointment is to see if there's anything actually wrong or not, so we'll just have to wait it out and not worry because there's nothing we can do. We'll just have to take it day-by-day if anything does need to be done! We love you Little One. Know that—no matter what!

*****

JOHN couldn't make it to the appointment immediately following the ultrasound; I mentally took notes so he could look it up when he got home. After asking the preliminary questions, the doctor took a deep breath and looked me in the eye. "It's getting later into your pregnancy, and we're going to need to know, will you want to continue with this pregnancy if—"

I cut her off, placing my hands over my wee one, hoping I was covering its ears. A baby should never hear such a question! "We will have this baby and love this baby no matter what, yes."

The doctor's eyes softened in a look that could only be relief. "I'm sorry; I have to ask that because some people—"

Apparently, I'm good at interrupting because I did it again. "No, it's okay. I understand. But not us. Not us."

Being a healthcare professional, John had all sorts of handy resources for looking up health questions. Me being me, all I could remember was: "It has something to do with the great vessels? She said it looks like his heart isn't doing something right with the blood flow, but they can't tell for sure until they do an echocardiogram. Is it serious? I mean, if that's what it ends up being?"

John pulled out his little hand-held gadget and tapped away. "Yeah. It could be big. But we don't know for sure." He explained

23

it to me, saying words that the doctor had used. At least I had told him the right info! And I had to agree.

"Nope, we don't know for sure."

That night, I made a phone call. "Sarah, it could be something big; but, it might not be."

"Oh, Hannie. What can we do?"

"Nothing. I mean we don't know anything yet. So I guess think good thoughts for us—to let the right things happen. But we're not telling anyone until we know more. We don't want to have people worried when we're out there for Seth's wedding. Okay?"

"Okay. Han?"

"Yeah?"

"I love you."

*****

7-18-06

MY HOPES FOR YOU: That you know how loved and cherished you are (already!), that you can be strong and tough when needed, and that you balance that with being soft and bending as well. There is strength in both! I hope that you are inspired by the light and beauty around and within you, that you seek knowledge, adventure, and love. That you are secure in who you are and where you want to go in your life. That you are full of spark and spunk and joy and humor! I love you, darling, for being your own unique, wonderful self.

My hopes and dreams for me: That I learn all I can from this life, that I am the best mom I can be, the best person I can be, and that I learn PATIENCE! I hope to have a sense of humor, wonderment, and hope for the present and the future. I hope that I am loved and respected by those I care about.

~*~

I HOPE YOU WILL BE a part of a team and learn how to be with other people. I hope you will be able to stand on your own and not need other people. I hope you will have the types of adventures (wild or mundane) that appeal to you and your nature. I hope you will

24

experience the heart-pounding rush and comfort of love (giving and receiving it). I hope you will see magic around you and miracles in little things. I hope you find true and selfless friendships. I hope you achieve what you want in life.

~*~

IF I COULD CHANGE THE WORLD, I would change it so that people are admired and emulated for the good that they do and the love that they spread, rather than what they look like or how much money they have. It really bugs me that sports players and actors get paid millions while other people, like teachers, childcare providers, social workers—even librarians and their libraries—make so little. These are the people who are raising the next generation of leaders, but they get nothing. Seems backwards to me.

And money's crazy, too. People keep earning more as the years go by, but then everything else (food, gas, homes, etc.) gets more expensive as well. So it all comes out equal in the end, but meanwhile everything keeps going up, up, up!

I'd want schools to improve and not be about test scores, but to be about learning and teaching in ways that excite and bring meaning and relevance to the students.

I'd like violence and bad things to just stop. I'd like there to be more fields of wildflowers for everyone to enjoy … and fewer blacktops, cars, and buildings. I'd like enough food, clothes, love, and laughter for everyone.

~*~

HAH, THIS MIGHT MAKE YOU SMILE! The best compliment I've received so far during this pregnancy is my eye rash is looking better! Seriously, that was what I was told. Hoo-boy! But, I don't feel blue, and I don't need compliments to make me smile. Oh, I crack myself up!

7-18-06

MY GOALS ARE SO BASIC. I just want to be cozy and peaceful in myself and my life. Silly as it may sound to you, I've always just wanted my own family (I've got it), my own space (got that, too), and time to sit down and read (even got that!). I'm such a homebody; I think I could probably BE anywhere, as long as it feels like home.

~*~

I LOVE WHEN Poppy lets me sleep in!

7-25-06

YOU ARE (maybe!) almost twenty-three weeks along! I think the doctors are using November 20th as the due date now (that's down from December 7th and November 24th!) You are moving around so much now and I can feel you thumping around on all sides of my belly! That makes me feel good. I want you to be as strong and healthy as possible! I really want to have our August 16 appointment so we can see what, if anything, is going on with your heart. There's a lot to know!

~*~

WOULD YOU LIKE TO KNOW about where we live? Well, we just moved here. I don't know all the ins and outs, but the Creston/Kalispell area seems like a nice spot to be. It's a pretty small town, with lots of gorgeous land and views from where we live. Glacier National Park is just a half-hour away. The people here are laid back and easygoing. I'll need to get used to not being so hurried! I think the downtown area is cute. I like the library, but need to find the good restaurants and parks still. Also, the stores are different—can't get all the shopping done in one place, because one store doesn't have it all! The people seem nice, the area feels comforting, and the potential for "our" spot is wonderful! And the whole area gorgeous!

August

8-7-06

YOUR ROOM IS FINISHED! Mostly. We still have computer stuff around and need to hang curtains and some pictures. But it's a good start.

8-15-06

I GOT TWO NICE COMPLIMENTS during the Wedding Trip: one from Poppy who looked at me as I modeled my outfit for Uncle Seth's wedding and said, "That is way cute." And one from a female stranger in the bathroom (of all places!) at Zephyr Cove (Lake Tahoe, California) when I was washing my hands. I was wearing my bathing suit and shorts, and she looked at me tugging at the outfit over my belly, smiled, and said "Cute!" So there you have it! (I actually prefer "cute" over "pretty"—sounds a little spunkier to me.)

~*~

YOUR JOURNAL IS GOING TO BE all hodge-podge and jumpy-around, but I guess that's how my mind works! Anyway, I just wanted to write that tomorrow we meet with the heart specialist for an echocardiogram to see how you're doing. I hope … so much I just *hope*, I suppose. You have been so active; especially at night; sometimes you even wake me up in middle of the night and keep me up for around an hour!

8-16-06

I WOULDN'T SAY I'M SCARED; worried might be right—more concerned about your safety than anything. We just had confirmation that your heart needs some help. You have what's called "Transposition of the Great Vessels," which basically means that your heart "tubing" is switched around. Oxygenated blood will circulate through your lungs while non-oxygenated blood will circulate throughout your body. So, now you will be born in Portland, Oregon, where some of the best surgeons will operate on your wee heart within a week after your birth.

It's around twelve hours to drive there and we should arrive when we're around thirty-seven to thirty-eight weeks (roughly the first week of November). If all goes well, we'll be there around four weeks! We're planning on taking the train. My goodness, what a way to greet the world! We still have ALL the details to figure out, but we're planning on moving the family to Portland for the whole time we need to be there! I can't even imagine what it will be like, but I do feel calm about it because whatever will happen, WILL happen. The doctors know what they're doing, and, by golly, I hope you'll be okay. I love you so much, Little One.

*****

THAT night I made another call. "It is what it is." That's how I greeted her and I said nothing else. She'd been waiting for the news.

Sarah's quiet intake of breath let me know she understood.

*****

8-16-06

WE'RE NOT FINDING OUT if you are a boy or girl because we want to be surprised! It's that last special treat of pregnancy, the first amazing part of your external life. This time we're secretly thinking you may be a boy because of your heart issue (two out of three with the condition are boys), so we'll be even more surprised if you're a girl. Either way, it's just too exciting and we can't wait to meet you!

~*~

WE STILL GO OUT for a three-mile run every day (missed a week while in California, and I feel bleh now). I love running. It gets me going in the morning, makes me feel happy, gets the kids outside, and introduces them to healthy habits. I listen to my body (and yours within me) to make sure I don't overdo it. We've met some really nice people and seen really neat animals—deer, humming birds, blue birds, horses, foxes, and "mystery" birds that look like a mix of turkey and pheasant!

8-17-06

THE FUNNIEST THING HAPPENED at the airport on our way home from Uncle Seth's wedding. Ellie, Mikey, and I were all together while I was using the potty (yup, there's that lack of privacy thing I mentioned before), when Mikey realized for the first time how to unlock a cubical door. Oh, yes, he did. With me yet to pull up my shorts, he was out the door and past the sinks. Without even zipping or washing, I was after him with Ellie at my side, practically rolling with laughter. I had to shout for someone to stop him before he made it all the way out of the bathroom! Whew, it was too funny. When you're a parent, all inhibitions go out the door!

~*~

SHORTLY AFTER MEETING POPPY, I started listening to country music—which I had never liked but which he did. I realized the songs made me think about him, so I started listening more closely to the words, and really thought the music was good, fun, and even inspirational. That's what I've been listening to since. There are so many songs that I totally love and all sorts of artists that I think are good.

One of my favorites right now has a line about "If you're going through hell, don't slow down. Just keep on moving ...." And I totally agree. You just have to keep on going with your life because what else would be the point? Many country songs have that theme or talk about things that are actually important, like family.

~*~

WE'D LIKE TO PAINT, but I haven't decided on a color yet! Your changing table is all set up and even has diapers. What size diapers will you be wearing when you come home? We may have stocked a size too small!

8-18-06

OKAY, what things am I looking forward to? The main thing, of course, is bringing you home. Then, your life!

8-20-06

WHAT WITH THE HEART STUFF that we've found out, I've realized how similar your Poppy and I are in our thoughts and rationalizations. Essentially that there's no use in freaking out or getting upset, as it would not help and would just be an endless, exhausting loop. Perhaps I feel even closer to him, can see more clearly how much we mean to him and how tender, thoughtful, and loving he is. Our brains seem to connect a bunch, and he'll end up calling me at the same time I think I should give him a call. He's a good man, your Poppy!

~*~

THOUGH I LOVE VACATIONS (who doesn't???), we haven't really taken any for a while; life kinda interferes. I'm counting our trip to Uncle Seth and Aunt Nikki's wedding (August 10th to the 15th) in Lake Tahoe, California, followed by a visit to Mr. Mike and Ms. Amy and their two girls in Sacramento, as a vacation. It was an awesome trip; Ellie was a flower girl! I'd really love to take us somewhere fun, like Hawaii—but I shouldn't be doing far away traveling right now.

September

9-2-06

YOU HAVE BEEN MOVING now for months!!! You are very active at night, waking me up or keeping me up—but I LOVE it. Ellie has felt you move now, too, and her eyes just light up and get huge when you give her hand a huge wallop! Poppy says he can feel you bopping around against his arm as he falls asleep. It's so neat that it seems like you're already here with us, a part of the family. It's a nice calm time, too—knowing that you're safe and snug inside me and haven't yet experienced crazy things, like heart surgery. I can see you move through my shirts and you can jiggle things resting on my tummy. Like ice cream bowls. You get the hiccups almost every night!

~*~

I PICTURE BRINGING YOU HOME and rocking you in the chair in your room ....

9-16-06

SWEETS. I want sweets. It is *so* bad!

~*~

OUR TYPICAL DAYS consist of getting your brother and sister ready for the day, putting out the doggy, Shilah, and going for a run. Then, we either play or do the shopping. After that comes lunch and then naps—all around! Then we have play/art/etc. time, followed by dinner, baths, and bed. Pretty basic, but it keeps us busy!

~*~

THERE HAVE BEEN LOTS and lots of doctors and nurses to talk to this time because of your wee heart. Things are starting to come together and we have "visiting" appointments coming up on October 4th and October 5th to meet the doctors and see the facility in Portland. All the doctors have been super nice and, at every appointment (boy, do we have a lot of those!), they all say how strong your heartbeat sounds, which is great. We want it to be as strong as possible!

~*~

A COUPLE OF THE MOMS that I admire most are my friends Kim and Krista. They are both raising children (two each) with love, respect, and compassion. Trying to have a balance of family and self. I love and respect them and the choices they have made for their families.

~*~

I WANT TO CREATE, for each of you, a childhood with memories that are full of magic, happiness, and creativity. I hope to build a foundation that is strong enough for you to build on for the rest of your life. I feel my parents did this for me.

~*~

AS I FALL ASLEEP AT NIGHT, my last thoughts are of you! Not just because I love you and you are often in my thoughts, but also because you move so much, it's hard to think of anything else. ;-)

~*~

THE WEATHER HAS JUST STARTED to cool down a ton and, for the next couple of days, we have rain and snow in the forecast. I love when it's all gray and cloudy. The grass looks very green against it, and the mountains are so majestic. Everything is all warm and homey inside. I've been feeling great and you've been moving tons!

9-17-06

WE ARE PLANNING TO HAVE Aunt Sarah (with Uncle Scott and Lucas) with us for the first week in Oregon, then Grandpa Mike for a week, and then Grandma Betsy for two weeks. They'll help with Ellie and Mikey while Mommy and Poppy are with you.

~*~

WEEKENDS IN OUR HOUSEHOLD are the same as the rest of the week—what changes is when Poppy's home (he works eight days and then is off for six). We typically go out to breakfast on one day, and then Ellie and Mikey like to hang out wherever Poppy is—which right now is usually somewhere working on some part of the house (which still isn't quite finished!)

~*~

SO FAR, a new car seat is all we've had to buy! We've got so many toys and clothes that we're kind of waiting to see who you are and what you like before we buy things specifically for you.

9-24-06

WE FOUND OUT on September 22nd that the doctors are planning your birth for some time between November 10th and November 15th. We will take the train on the evening of November 8th and arrive in Portland, Oregon, on November 9th. We are hoping to be there around a month (time for birth, surgery, and recovery). We will visit from October 2nd through October 5th to meet the doctors, see the facility, get an idea of the area, etc. We're looking forward to the trip!

~*~

IF I EVER GO BACK TO WORK, I'd like to teach or something along that line. A "dream" job (a nice idea, but I probably won't follow through with it) would be something in illustration. Right now, I'm a mama, and that's exactly what I want to be.

~*~

We love the location of our house; it's just across from the mountains, with wheat fields all around. It is so beautiful and peaceful here. On our runs in the morning, we see the sky/mountains/fields look a hundred different ways, and they're all magnificent! The actual neighborhood is unfinished with five inhabited homes (including ours), two houses up for sale, and around six empty two-acre lots.

9-26-06

Names! If you're a girl, your name will be Olivia Joy, named after your Great Grandma Joy. If you're a boy, we're thinking Clinton James (but we're not sure yet!)

~*~

Our house is transforming into a nice home. We've used mainly neutral colors with pops of sage and cranberry. We want to paint the bedrooms (even have the paint!), but haven't gotten around to it yet. We even have grass now—Poppy did all the sprinklers and grass seeding on his own! Outside our living room window, we have our land, then farmland (wheat fields), and then the huge, majestic mountains. It's beautiful—peaceful and always changing with the lighting and the weather! Poppy usually takes care of the outside chore stuff, while I do the inside things, but we don't limit ourselves to those roles and we help each other out regardless of what the job is.

October

10-5-06

TODAY, I HAD A DOCTOR'S APPOINTMENT, and I'm 33-½ weeks pregnant. This was the second day of appointments in Portland, and we met with the perinatologist—a super nice lady (everyone has been amazingly friendly, happy, and down to earth!). We found out I'm already 1-½ centimeters dilated! So ... they've moved the dates up a bit. We'll go to Portland on November 3rd via train, have an appointment on the 6th, get induced on the 8th at five a.m., and then, if all goes well, get you into surgery on the 13th. Can you believe it? The time is just disappearing. I hope you are ready, Little One; you're going to come into this world with a bang!

*****

"ARE you ready for what you'll need to deal with when you get back home?" Amy's voice is clear and upbeat, her nursing career waving a cheerful hello from her vocal chords. "Because there will be lots of doctor appointments at first, and medications ...."

"Hmm, actually I haven't thought much beyond this first step of getting us set to get out there. I think it's how I'm dealing with everything—just taking it all one step at a time."

"Okay, but if you're going to need help with anything, just let us know. I can always come up there if you need extra help with the baby's care."

*****

10-07-06

Now we're planning to name you Clinton Jacob, if you're a boy. Love it! Think that one's a keeper!

10-16-06

When I look in the mirror, I see a big, round, basketball belly! You are just so centered in there; it's easy to feel all sorts of little nobs and bumps—especially your heels!

~*~

We've got your other baby gear set up now, too! Highchair, bouncy seat, swing, cradle!

~*~

Aunt sarah, grandpa mike, and grandma betsy are all officially scheduled to come out and help before, during, and after your birth, so we won't have to worry about your older siblings while we're coming and going. Grandpa Miles and Grandma Nana are also planning to visit and offer their support.

10-17-06

We just came back from our trip to Portland, Oregon. We rode in an airplane, which was a thrill for Mikey and Ellie. Grandpa Mike came with us, to be with the kiddos while we did some hospital tours. Now, we have met all of the doctors, surgeons, nurses, etc., who will be helping you. We had a tour of where you'll be at the various stages of birth, surgery, and recovery. Then, they went over the details of the surgery. Sooo much information. I'm glad Poppy was there to help remember all the details.

On October 4th, they did the echocardiogram (a scan kind of like an ultrasound) and found that you also have a hole in the lower part of your heart, which could actually be helpful if it's big enough to allow your blood to mix before your surgery date. It adds to the risk and length of time for the surgery, but the doctor actually seems pleased that it's there (if "pleased" is the right word for it)! All of the doctors are incredibly nice and upbeat.

The plan has changed a bit, too, as I'm already beginning to dilate. Now the kids and I are taking the train on our own, leaving on November 2nd; Poppy will drive the car. That way we can bring more stuff and have our own car, instead of needing to rent one for so long. I'll still be induced on the morning of the 8th and you'll have your surgery on the 13th if all goes well! Then comes the wait for recovery. Oh, Honey, please be strong for us! We'll be strong for you, too.

~*~

OY, MY BELLY has become larger, I think! (Tee-hee!)

~*~

WITH THIS PREGNANCY, I haven't been very uncomfortable at all and don't feel very large or anything. I can certainly still function and get myself dressed. Could you imagine if I couldn't?! Sometimes it is hard to roll over in bed, but that's about it! I suppose that's when I feel the most pregnant. I'm not allowed to run anymore, but I can still walk for exercise!

~*~

MOST PREGNANT MAMAS PACK a suitcase to be prepared to rush to the hospital when the need arises. A suitcase? Ha! We've started packing and have got three tote boxes thus far. We'll be out there about a month, so I'm trying to think of everything you, the kids, and I will need over all that time!

We have about two-and-a-half weeks left before we start our journey! We found a furnished three bed/one bath cottage house a few miles from the hospital. We'll stay there with the family members who are coming to help us. What a crazy adventure!

10-22-06
WE'VE SET UP your car seat, and we've bought a new baby bath, too!

10-25-06

MY PACKED BAGS have climbed to four totes, one huge suitcase, two little suitcases for the kids, extra pillows, three blow-up mattresses, your car seat, and MORE!!!!!

*****

My sister was a good listener; I could talk to her about anything. "I'm feeling positive. We're as set as we can be. But ...." I hesitate.
"But, what?"
"Well, when I'm feeling not so positive.... Okay: How do you tell a three-year-old kid her baby might not come home?" I was sitting against the wall across from Ellie's door, at the top of the stairs. I looked down to the wooden floor below, waiting for an answer.
"I don't know, Han. But you'll know what to say, whatever it is, whenever the time is right."

*****

From: JohnandHannah@email.com
To: Krista@email.com
Sent: Saturday, October 28, 2006
Subject: Hello!

Hi Krista! What's new with you? I hope all is going well. I think you mentioned your sister was due around the same time as me? Is she doing okay this go round?

My sister Sarah just found out their second is a girl, due March 8th. Exciting for them.

We are almost done packing, and yesterday we visited the train station to get our bearings. A very cute, little station with about six wooden benches and a black and white tiled floor. The kids and I will be fine!

We decided John should drive our car to Portland; it's simpler than renting one for a month, and much cheaper. The kids and I are going via sleeper car, which is too exciting to think about!!!! Ellie is too cute about it.

We leave Thursday night. We're planning to bring our laptop with us, so if we can find a hook-up, I can keep you updated with emails. So far they're still planning to induce me on the 8th, and do the baby's surgery on the 13th.

Ellie has me nervous because she has had a strange stomach flu thing going on for the past couple of days—she looks so pale and bony now! I want her feeling better, and I don't want any of us to get it!

We went to the kids' school (well, it will be theirs when they're older) Halloween carnival, and have gone several times to a local pumpkin patch that has all sorts of activities set up for the kiddos. They are both going to be doggies this year—too cute!

Welp, I'm supposed to be napping now, so I should go!

Love you lots,

Hannah

~~~

November

From: JohnandHannah@email.com
To: Krista@email.com
Sent: Thursday, November 2, 2006
Subject: Hi

Dear Krista,

It was so good to hear from you! We are really, actually, doing well. It is soooooo out of our hands, and we can only take one day at a time (which is actually helpful), and what happens will happen. We are confident in the surgeon and other doctors and know they will do the best job possible. We can't ask for more.

It's just hit me that I'm supposed to have this wee one in a week! I have been so focused on the first steps—the packing, cleaning, and setting up of who is coming when—that the reason has been pushed to the back of my mind. About a week or two ago, we got our baby gear from storage (though the room has been set up since we moved in), and that really made me realize it's almost time! So, now I'm starting to think about the actual labor and don't know what to expect (do we ever?!) because I may not be as far along as I was with the other two—a longer labor for me??

After that, when we know how the baby is doing, I'll be able to start thinking about the next step. There are so many unknowns. I just had another ultrasound, and they think the baby is only five pounds, ten ounces. We're hoping it's just a small baby and not a premature baby, as that could bring along lung issues. They still think the dates are right, though, and my body is doing everything it should be doing at thirty-seven weeks of pregnancy.

This baby cracks me up. It's so busy poking and jabbing and "rising to the surface," as I call it (when the baby bulges randomly on one side of my belly, making me lopsided). It gets the hiccups at least once a day. It's so cute and sweet and dear to me already. No matter the outcome of all this, I have already been blessed with this wee one's "just being." We'll let you know if the dates change.

I was right to be worried about Ellie. John brought her to the ER on Sunday because she just wasn't right. It ended up she was dehydrated and they had to hook her up to an IV and give her two bags of fluids! She is doing much better now.

The kids are really looking forward to this trip; we're trying to keep it as fun and adventurous as possible for them. We leave tomorrow on the 9:10 p.m. train and arrive in Portland at 10:25 a.m. I should be going now. Wish us luck!

Love,

Hannah

~~~

11-4-06

IN EARLY OCTOBER, we had a quick tour of Oregon Health and Science University (OHSU), where I will have you, and Doernbecher, the children's hospital you'll go to for your surgery and recovery. Huge facilities! OHSU is a teaching hospital. That means there's all different levels of experience these doctors have had; some are still students going on rotations, and it goes all the way up to people with several years of residency and such.

We met a lot of doctors and other personnel; everyone is great—super smart and kind. We were shown the various rooms you will be in for waiting, surgery, and recovery—saw a bunch of cute babies, too. Can't wait to see you!!!! Haven't seen the birthing area yet—should try on Monday when we have an appointment!

THE HOSPITAL, AS SEEN FROM OUR ROOM

11-5-06

WE MADE IT TO PORTLAND! The kids and I took the train while Poppy drove. It was very exciting—like a movie when we left, with huge soap-bubble snowflakes coming down. We had a sleeper berth and went to bed when we boarded. In the morning, we had the most gorgeous views. Picture us. Here I am, days away from delivery, lugging two car seats, a large duffel bag, and two kids wearing coats and pajamas. And neither of them are feeling their best. Ellie just had a short ER visit less than a week ago, and Mikey got flu-sick on our train ride and slept from breakfast until our train arrived after lunchtime!

It really was a blast, though—a trip I don't think any of us will ever forget. None of us had traveled overnight on a train before. What an eventful, fun, and crazy way to start the adventure of You!

We arrived yesterday and did "spring cleaning" in the house, a cottage we have rented fully furnished. We've got things all set up, and now Poppy is grocery shopping. Tomorrow, Aunt Sarah and her family are coming and, on Monday, we have our last regular appointment!

~*~

I THINK KEEPING UP with things dear to us is important right now. I've been rereading the Agatha Christie books, something I find quite enjoyable. I own them all and have read them a ton—but they're so good!

~*~

MY DREAMS ARE ALWAYS CRAZY, wacky, and vivid. Sometimes I think they'd make good books or movies! At the beginning of the pregnancy, a common theme was being at school or working at Longs Drugs (which is where I met Poppy forever ago). Now it's completely random.

I go to bed too late, usually because I'm reading, and wake up earlyish with the kids (around six or seven a.m.). I try to take an afternoon nap (but sometimes read through it). I'm often really tired around lunch time, but then feel too awake at bedtime! If I really can't sleep at night (like when you wake me up with all your moving around), I usually get a little snack and a book and sit out in the living room.

~*~

SOME SIMPLE WANTS I HAVE FOR US: I want us to be a happy family. I want holidays to be yummy and magical—something you enjoy and like to remember and isn't all about stress and who gets along best with who. I want us to eat meals together and share each other's company. I want to have activities, outings, and adventures together. I want you to grow up and still like us and have fond memories of your childhood. And it would be perfect, when you're grown up, if you still want to be a part of your crazy family and not feel like you have to be a part of it!

A HAPPY FAMILY, BUILT ON LOVE

11-7-06

WE HAD AN APPOINTMENT yesterday and found out I was 4 cm and 50% effaced, so I was hooked up to monitors. They found I was having contractions I couldn't feel, around six minutes apart. They sent me to Labor and Delivery, just in case, and checked me again. Still 4 cm, but now I was 75% effaced, and for a bit was having contractions four minutes apart. No further changes, so they unhooked us and we were able to leave at 5:30 (had been there since 11:30 for our appointment!). They decided to push the date of your delivery to the 10th, unless you come earlier on your own!

11-9-06

THIS IS IT, Little One! We'll be going this evening at midnight, and they should start things at five a.m. on the 10th. Just wanted to let you know we all love you so much—have been getting prayers and well-wishes from people we don't even know! We wish you the best and hope things work out as they should. No matter what, we will always love you.

Almost Time

Letters

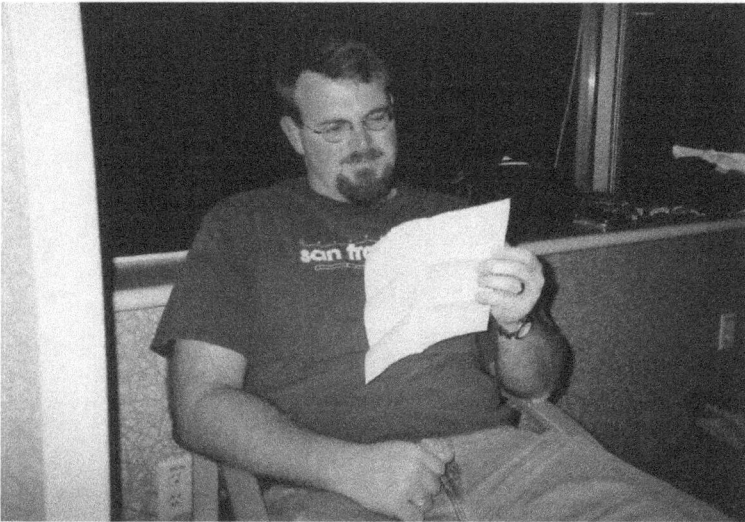

POPPY READING HIS LETTER FROM MOMMY

11-10-06

Dear John,

Well, here we are for the third time! New state, new job, new child ... don't we go in for the BIG changes?! I love you so much, Honey. You are a wonderful person—so sweet and caring as a father, a husband, a friend. We are all so lucky to have you. And

46

now with this new Wee Sullivan and everything that has been going on, and will be going on, and may be going on …! Thank you for being so calm and normal and matter-of-fact.

Whatever we face, we shall handle it together and be the stronger for it. What an adventure it is, and I am so glad to be going on it with you. I admire and respect you so much and think the kids will do so well in life having you as a role model.

So grip my hand tight and breathe me through this and let us show everyone how it's done! Since we had to come all the way out here, we may as well give them a show! I love you, Honeybunch! Thanks for being such a darling Poppy.

Love, me

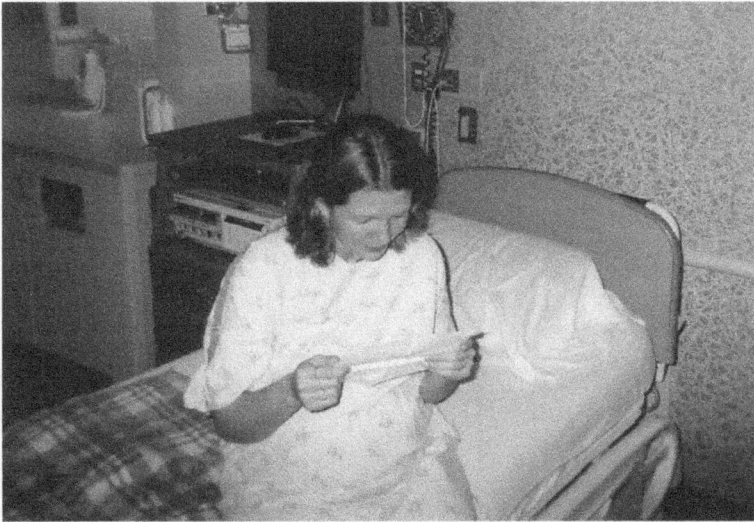

MOMMY READING HER LETTER FROM POPPY

11-10-06

To My Dearest Wife,

Let me first start by saying I love you so much. You are the most wonderful person I know. You are the most wonderful mother I know. I have never met anyone who is as wonderful with children as you are. We have been faced with many challenges in our lifetime together. We have always said we can't wait for what life has in store for us. This will be our biggest challenge yet, and I feel that we will take this in full stride, as we have in the past, and become stronger and closer than ever. There is not another person in the world that I would want by my side other than you. Please know that I am here for you to laugh with, love with, and cry with. We will embark on a whirlwind of emotions. Please know that I am here for anything. I love you with all my heart. Be strong when you need to be, but remember to let it go when you need to as well.

I love you.
XOXOXO
John

Precious Life

A Baby Is Born

11-10-06

BABY BOY! Clinton Jacob! You were born TODAY at 11:26 a.m. at OHSU in Portland, Oregon!!!

We went in at midnight, as the doctor ordered, in preparation for your five a.m. induction. The time was changed when they realized the team of doctors you'd need wouldn't arrive until eight a.m. This would be too late for your arrival, based on the speed of my previous labors. They broke my water, the only induction procedure I've ever needed, around 8:20.

I was having contractions, but wasn't feeling any, so Poppy and I walked and walked loops through the hallways. Your monitors, picking up my vitals instead of yours, kept beeping like crazy! Finally, I started to feel them, and soon thereafter was feeling them strong enough to want to stay in our room to walk around. At that point, I was having contractions every two minutes, and before long I said I needed to climb into bed.

Not much later, I knew you were coming! I overheard a nurse say to the other team members that they should gather everyone because she thought you would be born "within an hour." A doctor said, "Wow, she was walking the hallways just twenty minutes ago, and now she's almost ready. I have a feeling this baby is going to come quickly."

I knew you were coming quickly, so I whispered to Poppy to get people IN. They came right away (Poppy actually had to ask twice!), but I was almost scared they wouldn't be fast enough!

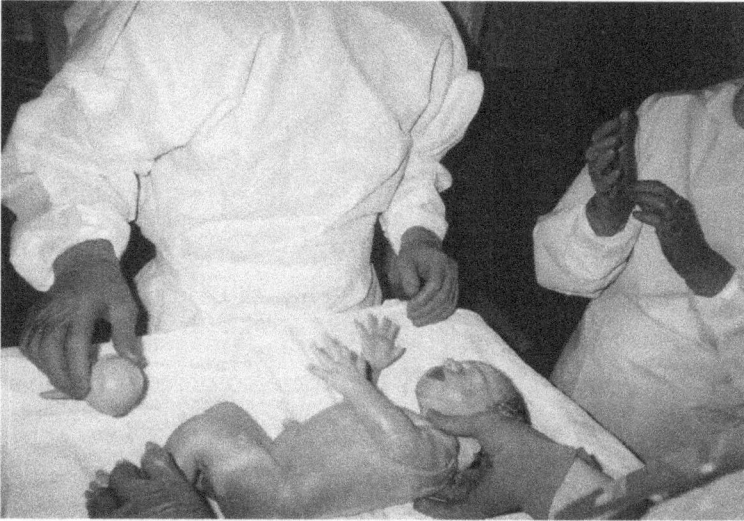

CLINTON, MOMENTS AFTER BIRTH

You had a whole team waiting for you! Two contractions and you were out, looking pink and strong—you even peed right in the air as you were passed from me to the waiting team. Too funny! They whisked you away to a special room to check your vitals and blood-oxygen levels. You were doing very well, so they brought you back to the room after they placed your line and IVs. You even nursed before you were taken to the Neonatal Intensive Care Unit (NICU).

There they found that the hole in your heart was smaller than originally thought, so this evening they ended up doing what they call the "balloon" procedure (ripping a hole in your heart to allow the blood to mix.) You did great! Welcome to the world!!!!

~*~

WE CALLED YOUR BROTHER AND SISTER first thing. I could hear Ellie in the background saying, "It's a bruver, it's a bruver!" Mikey kissed the phone, and then we talked to Sarah and Scott (who are on child-watch duty). They were so excited to hear about your arrival. After that, we called the rest of our family and friends. Everyone is thrilled that you have arrived—they send you their love and best wishes. Grandmas Nana and Betsy, Aunt Sarah, Uncle Scott (with Lucas), Ellie, and Mikey all came to visit you. Mikey kept repeating "Baybee Cinton!" Grandpa Miles tried to be here for your birth, but had to leave before you showed up.

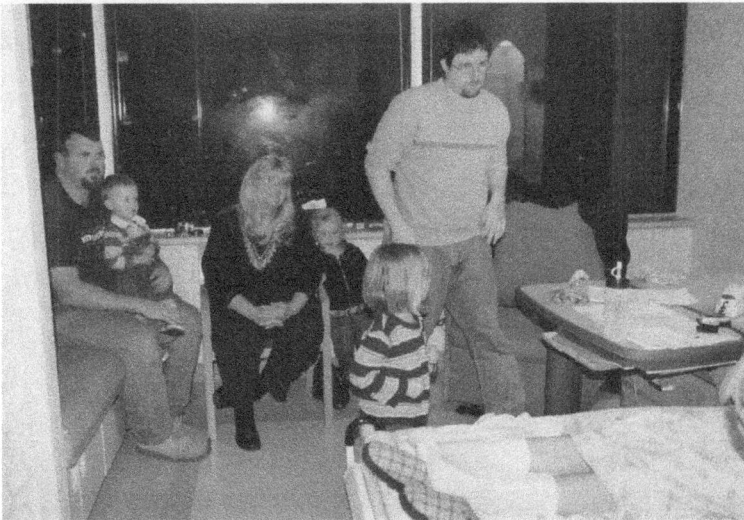

GRANDMA BETSY, UNCLE SCOTT, AND LUCAS VISIT US IN RECOVERY.

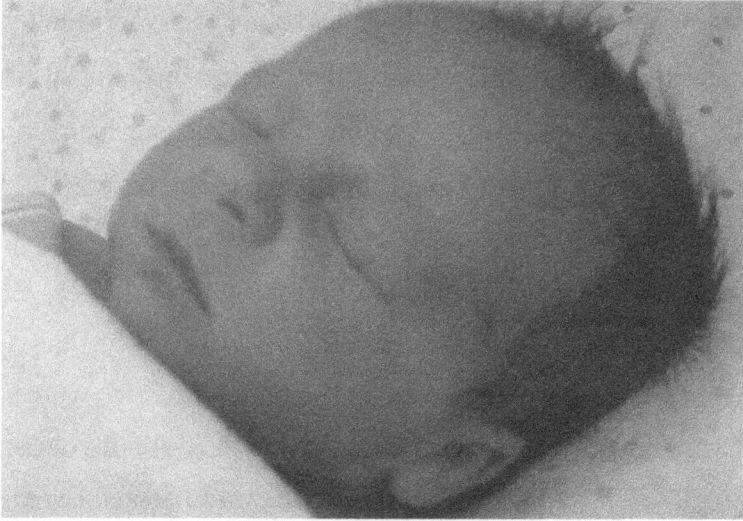

CLINTON JACOB SULLIVAN

11-11-06

YOU HAD TWO EPISODES of apnea this morning (probably because of the medications for last night's procedures), and you had to be intubated. They gave you Tylenol to help with pain, just in case that's why you stopped breathing. After that, you seemed stable. Yay!

You had two bottles today, and you nursed! First try, you just slept in my arms, sweet boy, and the second time, you ate for thirty minutes! You are precious, Honey, and we love you so very, very much! Forgot to write what you look like—tons of dark hair (almost black!) and a sweet little body—perfect and not even squished. You are six pounds, eleven ounces, and 19-¾ inches long. You had your eyes open right after you were born, but they haven't been open since.

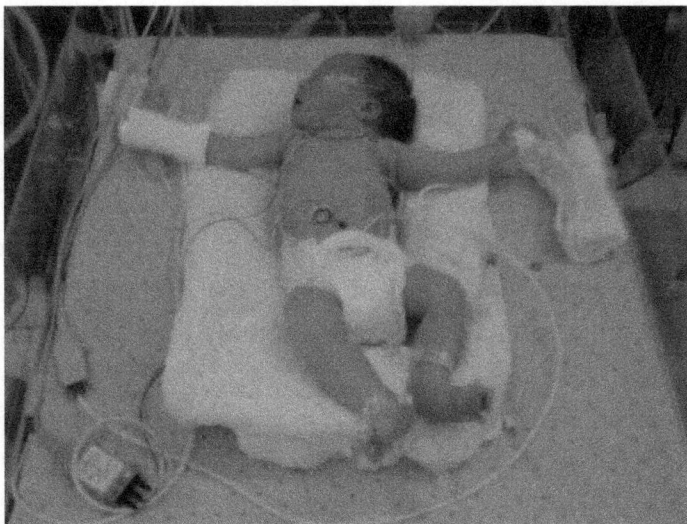

CLINTON, AFTER BEING INTUBATED

11-12-06

I WAS DISCHARGED TODAY, after staying as long as I was allowed. It's so odd to be walking out of the hospital without you. I don't like leaving you. I love you so much. We'll be coming back and forth now to visit, feed, and be with you. In the Neonatal Intensive Care Unit (NICU), there are no hospital-supplied sleeping areas for the parents. Each baby is in a bay of four infants and two nurses and there are only rocking chairs and stools for our use.

After surgery, you will be in the Pediatric Intensive Care Unit (PICU) and, as a risk level of 8—the highest, and given to all heart patients—you will be one-on-one with the nursing staff. We'll have a little bed for our use in that room. They told us many family members stay elsewhere, some just sleeping in chairs in the waiting room. When I asked why, I was told it was too hard for some people to be so close to everything going on; they need some degree of separation from the intensity. Also, it's hard to get sleep because the PICU floor is loud with beeps and alarms, the x-rays on the patients who need them are taken at five in the morning, and doctor rounds happen every morning at seven.

11-13-06

GRANDPA MIKE HAS ARRIVED to take over watching Ellie and Mikey (Sarah leaves tomorrow) and he came in to visit you. He couldn't get over how cute you are. You really are adorable with a nice round head, long monkey toes, precious ears that are a little pointy like an elf's, a button nose, and that soft, soft hair! Scrumptious. Grandpa sat in with us while a nurse practitioner went over more details of what to expect for the surgery. Lots of details. Poppy's friend, Mr. Mike, comes in late tonight. So many people are thinking of you.

~*~

YOU'VE BEEN MUCH MORE STABLE, though your blood/oxygen levels have been slightly decreasing daily. They decided to start you on Prostaglandin (a drug to keep your holes from closing), which makes you feel icky and cranky. I hold you on my lap and you fall asleep, and it makes all of your vitals even out a bit.

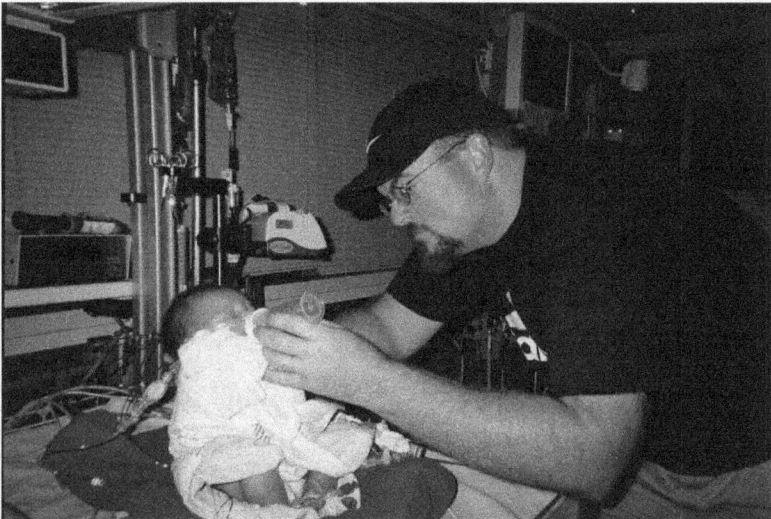

LATE-NIGHT MEALTIME

54

I've been pumping milk for you like crazy and nursing you when possible. You're so sweet. You've opened your eyes once or twice and cry with a cat's meow sound. Your hair is soft and fuzzy, almost an inch long! Poppy likes visiting you at night, when no one much is around. You're certainly a loved little boy. Tomorrow is your big day. Be strong, Small One. We love you!

Getting to the Heart of It

Looking Deep

11-14-06

The day! THE day! We arrived at six a.m. to hold and cuddle you and take some pictures together. You don't like getting your photo taken; the light of the flash makes you jump, so I haven't been taking as many as I would normally ….

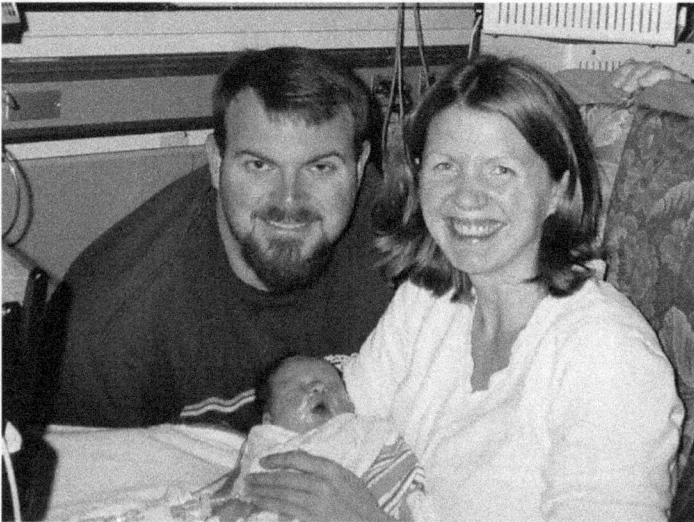

THE MORNING OF CLINTON'S SURGERY

They wheeled you (with us following) down to the surgery site at 7:20. There, the various anesthesiologists, doctors, etc. told us about what to expect during and after the procedure and what their overall plan was. We kissed you goodbye after heart-loads of "I love yous" and pep talks about being tough and strong and listening to your surgeon. Then we sent you off. We love you so much, Little One. Please do your best.

~*~

AT 8:53, they called the phone desk (we're currently sitting in the waiting room) to let us know they'd made the incision!

It's 9:30 and you've been put on bypass and they are working on your VSD/ASD (the extra hole). Things are moving quickly and well, they tell us.

Done with the VSD at eleven; now they're starting on the arterial switch.

As your surgery progresses, we are calling everyone again, to let them know how it's going; things are still going well.

At 12:10, they're all done with the repair and they have shut off the pumps. Around forty-five more minutes, then you're going to the PICU ….

*****

THE surgeon called the waiting room desk as opportunity arose, just to keep us updated. John and I sat, talking between the waiting. Sometimes the waiting is the hardest part of anything a person has to face; sometimes it's just long and tedious. We broke the monotony by chatting with other waiting parents, hearing snippets of other people's lives. Ellie and Mikey also came in for a quick visit.

John stepped out, and shortly afterwards, the surgeon arrived to talk to us. I followed him, alone, crossing my fingers John would make it back fast—he'd understand the surgeon better and would know what kind of questions to ask. All I wanted to know was: "Is my baby okay?" John came through the doors almost immediately, and I breathed easier.

*****

11-14-06

WELL, BY GOLLY, I've lost track of time! You were sent down to the PICU where they hooked you up to your machines and medications. After a while (around 2:something p.m.), they were set to have us come see you. Oh, Honey, you are BEAUTIFUL, my sweet little boy. You've got tubes and wires and machines all around you, but smack dab in the middle of it all is YOU, just shining through.

They say the first twelve hours are the most critical, and so far you seem to be holding pretty steady. I will be staying with you tonight and Poppy will stay tomorrow. Mr. Mike was here today and got to meet you, too. Grandpa Mike stopped by with Ellie and Mikey during the surgery, and then afterwards he came back on his own to visit with you. We're all amazed by you. Hang in there and be strong, Little One; we've still a ways to go.

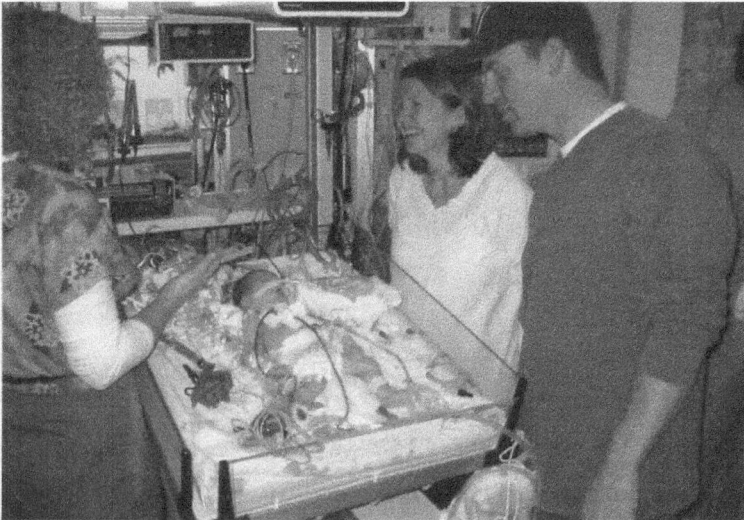

MR. MIKE COMES TO VISIT AFTER CLINTON'S SURGERY.

11-15-06 (from Poppy)

More recovery today. The staff worked hard to get you to pee. You seem to be close to getting over the hump for your heart to really start healing and improving output. We love you so much. It is hard not to be able to stay with you every minute. It is also very hard not to be with your brother and sister, too. They can't wait to get home and have you there as well. Your brother has your name down pretty well. Your sister and I still refer to you as Clinton Jacob Boomer Barley Sullivan. We all love you. Continue to be strong.

11-16-06

Sweetie, you are still doing well. Up and down in minor ways. You need to PEE! They'll be running various echoes, tests, and theories to see if they can figure out what is going on. We met the nicest couple in the waiting room the other day during your surgery. Their ten month old had heart surgery, too. We've been visiting back and forth. It's good to have friends around. We love you forever much. Hang in there and be tough, Little Guy. This won't last forever and we'll be able to hold and cuddle you soon.

*****

The child-life specialist came to me and asked if I'd be okay showing this new heart patient mom how to work the pump for her milk. Maybe we could visit with her and her husband, as the two were having a difficult time seeing their young son go through everything.

"Sure," I responded, not knowing if it was me or the other mom who would be helped the most by having contact with someone else.

*****

The Jump

Riding the Rollercoaster

11-16-06

YOU HAVE HAD A ROUGH DAY, Little One. Please hang tight and pull through. We love you so much. I am so sorry you have to go through this. You are extremely edematous—so swollen from third-spacing your fluids, rather than peeing. That means your fluids are moving into your body tissues instead of following the circulatory route they're supposed to. You are becoming toxic to yourself and have grown several times your regular size. It is typical for peeing to stop for a day or two after a big surgery, just due to the stress on the body. However, as in most all the routes that you're seeming to take, yours is an extreme case …. Oh, sweet Clinton!

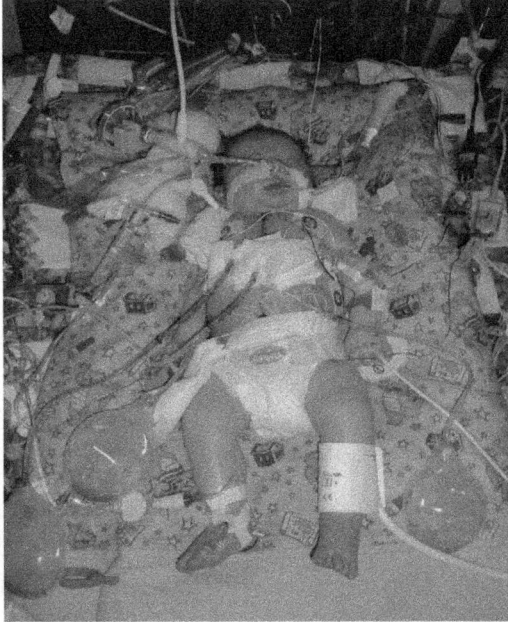

CLINTON BEGINNING TO SWELL

11-17-06

LAST NIGHT WAS THE LONGEST, scariest night of our lives. Yours, too. Oh, honey, all your rates were decreasing and decreasing. As one nurse put it: "We've been doing okay digging in sand and keeping him even. But not anymore. The sand is now coming faster than we can shovel."

They tried you on new drugs, gave a total of three echoes, took x-rays, and just couldn't figure it out. The beginning of the big drop seemed to be at 12:30 a.m. At 2:30 a.m., they came to me. I was "sleeping" in the bed, located just behind your bassinet and drug pumps, listening to what was happening, yet staying clear for them to work. They said they were calling the surgeon because they thought they knew the problem.

Since your surgery, your blood pressure has been way too low, your body tissues absorbing your fluids, your kidneys not getting enough fluids to make you pee, you poufing up because of all the fluid retention, and your body working too hard at not

61

accomplishing anything. A vicious cycle. So they thought, even though your heart was beating well, it just didn't have the strength to combat the pressure of your lungs, which couldn't push enough pressure to reach around your body. They let me know of a machine and a procedure they were going to try. If not, you weren't going to make it. Completely scary.

The surgeon agreed this was the way to go. They opened your chest again, and essentially put you on another bypass machine, called ECMO, which would work for you as your heart and lungs and kidneys if needed. Your blood (and extra blood) is oxygenated through the machine and cycled through your body. Your organ muscles will be worked enough to get them strengthened. The plan is to let you rest, recoup, get rid of all the medications in your body, fix all the previous cycle of issues, get you peeing (which would relieve the poufing), and then slowly wean you off the machine as your body gets stronger and can start doing it on its own.

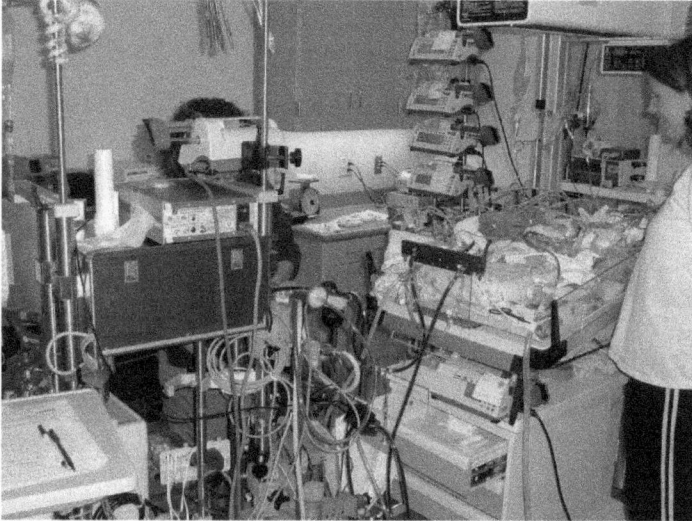

CLINTON ON ECMO

After they explained this to me, I called Poppy to give him the update. Those three miles to the hospital must have felt like forever. They did the procedure right there in your room, with Poppy and me pacing the hallways and waiting. The nurse later said, "He jumped off a cliff, but we grabbed him by the chains and pulled him back."

Oh, Little One. Be strong. Get your rest, exercise your muscles, be able to get off the machine …. We love you so much.

11-18-06

HAS IT REALLY ONLY BEEN TWO DAYS since your drop? You look so much better. You have been peeing a lot and much of your swelling has gone down. We can see the features and bone structure of your face again! I can actually watch the blood flow cycle from your body, into ECMO, and back again. They have already been lowering settings on the ECMO machine and have lowered the amount of venting you are receiving!

There are around-the-clock, fulltime nurses specially trained for ECMO, who have the job of literally sitting all day and night, just watching the machine. Which, along with your hospital bassinet and your stacked IV drug pump dispenser, takes up the entire middle strip of your room. Tubes and wires, attached-to-you suctioning bulbs, warmers for the cannulas (so the blood isn't too cold for you), stuffed animals to help hold everything away from your body … and YOU. And then you have separate nurses for yourself. That's how major the repercussions of anything going wrong with this treatment are. You get two nurses a day, for the day shift and the night shift.

You respond to our voices and touch: trying to turn your head when you hear us, opening your left eye (I've seen you open both a couple times now!), raising your arm, and wiggling your toes! Amazing. By the evening of the 16th, you hadn't been able to do any of that anymore, you were too swollen and sick.

11-20-06

EVERY TIME I SEE YOU, you look smaller! Seems an odd thing to want in a newborn. Grandma Betsy is here again (Grandpa Mike left yesterday), and Ellie and Mikey visited you again yesterday. Ellie asks so many questions about you and your tubes, etc. When she was here, she rubbed your little knee and asked me to kiss it for her.

Your legs/feet are clear of obstruction—just one monitor left on your foot. Your chest is still well hidden under tubes, pumps, wires, and swabs (did I write that your chest is still open?), but you look very restful. You wake up a bunch now, opening both eyes and trying to look around, lift your wrist, wiggle your toes, etc.

Last night I was touching your foot and you kept pressing back against my fingers. I love seeing you move, but feel a little wary about it—I don't want you to be too awake! Also, your alarms beep more because your heart rate goes up!

They started you on milk yesterday! It goes through a feeding tube in your mouth and means you're doing a little better, not needing all the medically created TPN (Total Parenteral Nutrition) stuff. You've got lots of tape going across your nose and cheek, holding your other tubes from getting knocked out of your nostrils. Gauze pads plume beneath your cheeks, fluting around your lower face/chin area, and making a bit of a stylistic ruff. They're thinking of weaning you from your ECMO machine around Wednesday. Thursday is Thanksgiving.

Oh, man, I love you.

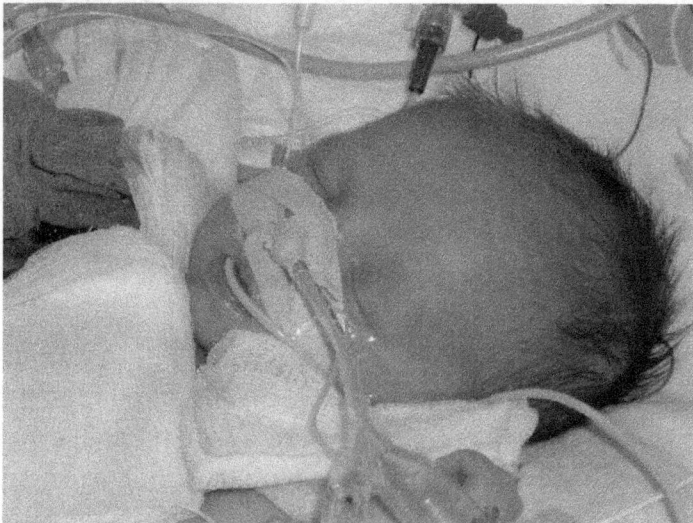

CLINTON WITH HIS FEEDING TUBE IN HIS MOUTH: MILK!

11-21-06

THEY'VE INCREASED your milk intake!

11-22-06

TODAY'S THE DAY, Little One! They're going to do a trial run with you off ECMO for a few hours (after decreasing it a bit more) and, if you do well, they'll keep you off and take your cannulas (blood flow tubes) out and sew up your chest. You have been very alert and active this morning, as if you know something's happening. Please, Little Guy, please do all right. Hold your ground and be strong. We love you so much.

~*~

YOU STAYED OFF for three hours! A good practice run, but not good enough for the real deal. Your pulmonary hypertension is still present. Little Guy, work on that. Please be strong and get well. We want to take you home. We love you.

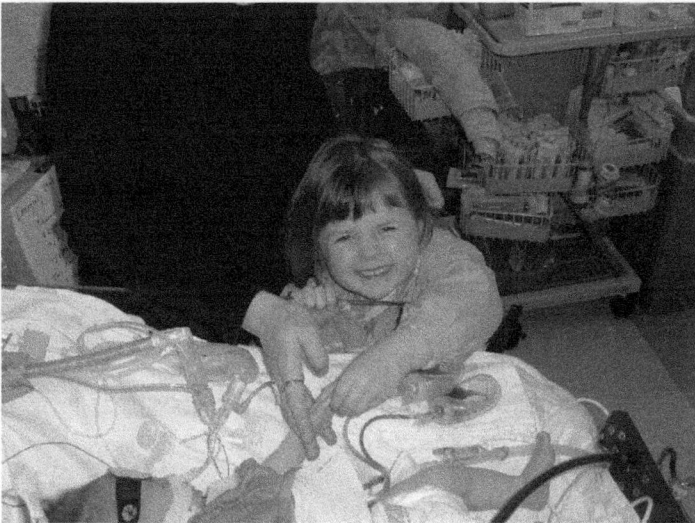

ELLIE ADORES HOLDING HANDS WITH CLINTON.

11-23-06

THANKSGIVING! We are thankful that you are in our lives and are a part of our family. We're especially thankful that Ellie and Mikey can be a part of your life here at the hospital. Even though they don't get to really live with you, they know you and know you are their baby brother. We love you so incredibly much.

11-24-06

YOU ARE two weeks old!

~*~

ANOTHER ROUGH NIGHT for you, Little One. You started to bleed out, a lot, and they thought perhaps a cannula had started to slip. They had to remove your chest patch to see what was going on and discovered that a blood vessel on the surface of your heart had begun to bleed. They fixed that in another in-room surgery. Then (with a HUGE procession, and us in tow) they got you down to the Cath Lab, so they can look more closely at your heart and lungs and see what is going on. You're still showing high pressures in your lungs. They hope to remove you from the ECMO machine sometime this weekend. You looked like such a real baby when they wheeled you and your equipment to the Cath Lab floor.

~*~

WHEW! Well, you went straight from Cath Lab to SURGERY. They found that one of your pulmonary arteries was way too tight and narrow, so the surgeon went back in and expanded it. After several hours you came back, WITHOUT ECMO!!! So far, your stats have been holding steady. They think that the stenosis is what caused all of the issues you've been dealing with since surgery. Poppy and I are both staying tonight.

THE FAMILY VISITS WITH CLINTON AND ONE OF THE BEST NURSES EVER.

11-25-06

WE HAVE BEEN "back-and-forthing" for two weeks now. We'll both be with you in the morning; usually go home for lunch and maybe a nap; come back to you; return home for dinner, bath, and bedtime for the kids; and then come back to you again. Ellie and Mikey visit you during the day, too, hanging out with Poppy and me—and all your amazing nurses. Typically, I get four hours of sleep at night.

We're getting to know the staff as family and the hospital as our second home, with you glowing in the center of all the craziness!

~*~

OVERNIGHT WITHOUT ECMO! You're doing very well—pressures are increasing, lactates decreasing, you're not paced right now .... Hmm, I don't think I've ever mentioned you have an external pace maker, to help make sure the rhythm of your heart stays strong and regular.

Buddy, we're all praying for you to keep it up. You have gone through so much; PLEASE make it the whole way! More (good) excitement today: You've had two poopies! Not much pee, yet, but you've had some, which is a good start. Also Miss Heidi's mom, Connie, who lives here, came to visit you in the hospital—the first non-family visitor (besides Mr. Mike, who's like family). Heidi is a friend from Idaho. She even brought surprises and goodies for us and the kiddos.

Ellie was able to kiss your foot today, and then Mikey did, too. They both like to rub your hair. Lots of people are falling in love with you. Some doctors have even been calling on their days off to see how you are doing. Ellie likes telling you things so you can "see" them even though your eyes are closed (like showing you her new mittens), and she also sings to you. Very sweet.

Heard today we could be here another month …. We'll see! Mikey will most likely be turning two here! I forgot to write that I've helped wash you two times now!

11-28-06

WELL, yesterday you still hadn't started to pee yet and had poufed up hugely (again), with numbers starting to climb, so they decided to get you on dialysis and they poked your belly with another tube in preparation. You lost a lot of fluid with that and shrunk in size a bit as well.

~~~

From: JohnandHannah@email.com
To: Krista@email.com
Sent: Wednesday, November 29, 2006
Subject: Whew!!!

Krista, it has been such a ride, so up and down, with nights where we were close to losing him, to days like this where he's been holding steady. He is so strong for a wee one! We love him so incredibly much; he is so sweet and cute. Even though he's only pretty much been sleeping, he has such character that the nurses argue over who gets to care for him. He's the youngest patient in there right now. It just rips my heart out when he's not doing well. The doctors feel positive right now (everything seems to change daily with Clinton, but the doctors probably know best) and say we can expect to stay for another month.

The kids are doing really well for the situation, with John and me back-and-forthing. Family members have made that possible. They've gone to the zoo, museum, and park! Our house here, we just found out yesterday, has been rented out already for the new time-frame, so John is house searching again. We may have found a furnished apartment—John will look at it tomorrow. We need to be out of ours on the 2nd! Mikey turns two on the 8th, and we may be here for Christmas!!! Crazy!!!

The people here are absolutely amazing: so loving, nurturing, and brilliant. We are in good hands. We know the best is being done, and Clinton is trying so hard. All we can do is sit back for the ride and hope. Hope, always. I love him sooooo much. Back to the awesomeness of this place, a nurse overheard me talking about Mikey's b'day and how his presents are at home (as are all the X-mas gifts!) and she brought me back to this room filled with donated toys, blankets, books, etc. and had me choose b'day gifts for him and some things for Ellie. I felt guilty for taking things because I don't feel needy, but the nurse said this is the reason for the toy room. She told me that I'm making the donors happy by taking the gifts, and then I can make other people happy by paying it forward and donating things when we get back to Montana. I like that idea, though I still feel a bit guilty!

Life has been crazy, but we are doing very well. The kids visit their brother and go on special trips with their grandma, etc. They see us either in the mornings or in the evenings. (We try to be there for the main parts of their day like dinner, bath, and bedtime.) Then I sleep at the hospital. I feel even closer to John and know we will get through this together absolutely. Write back to me! If you want to send a note or anything, use our Montana address. John's brother is picking up the mail, and eventually we will be home to receive it! I love you bunches and hope you are well!

Love, Hannah

~~~

December

12-1-06

BABY BOY! You are three weeks old now! So sweet. You're a little more alert, though still on a lot of meds to keep you sleepy and pain-free. You open your eyes and look around before they roll closed again. You also move your arms, hands, feet, and mouth, all silently and in slow motion, but very cute and promising, nonetheless! Did I write that your feeding tube was changed from your mouth to your nose, so now we can see your darling lips better? Precious. We love you forever and ever. And always!

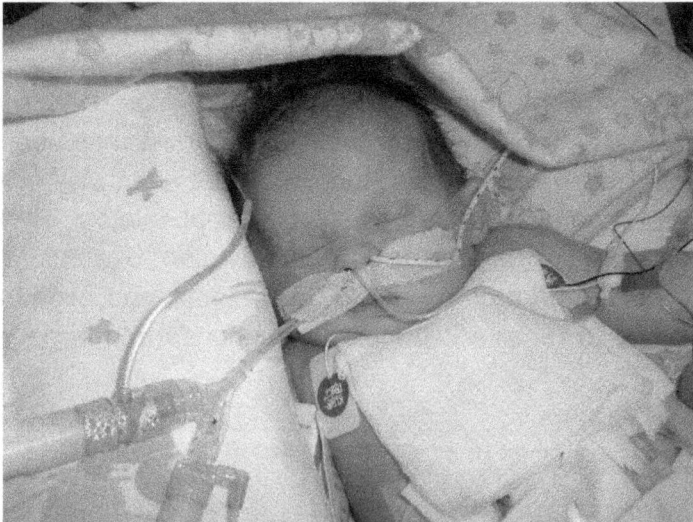

OUR SWEET BOY

~*~

You were put on peritoneal dialysis a day or so ago. It seems to be working—you're losing your extra fluid and your numbers are getting better balanced. You pee a little bit now and then, as well! Dopamine and Epinephrine have officially been weaned. You are paced off and on. OH! Totally forgot to write this: you had another CRAZY night two nights ago, just before being put on dialysis. Your heart started these crazy arrhythmias, beating up to 280 bpm, when your regular rate is around 120 bpm; it would barely slow down before going back at it …. They tried various drugs and then a combo of drugs and the pacer to out-beat your heart's rhythms and then slow it down. Finally, that process worked sometime in the morning …. You just have a patch over your heart/open chest, and I could actually see the frantic beating.

Oh, Little One, you are doing so well now, but there are still so many things that could happen or need to happen …. You have so many people concerned for you and praying for you! We love you so much. Ellie and Mikey like coming to visit you and give you pats, rubs, and kisses. Ellie tells me what part of your body to kiss when I'm coming in for the night. Mikey likes your head. Oh! Also forgot to write that your legs have huge blood clots and it's hard to find a pulse there.

*****

STEPPING into the hallway leading to the PICU, I saw an older woman, looking like how I felt. Though I knew the faces of almost everyone who came and went in this particular corner of the world, I did not recognize her. She met my eyes. "Do you have someone in there?" She gestured behind herself, to the bend in the hallway; beyond the corner was the check-in station. All visitors needed to be verified.

"Yeah." I pushed back my wet hair; I'd just taken a shower. "He's the youngest kiddo in there right now. Do you have someone, too?" I was cautious in asking; she looked so fragile.

"Yes; my grandson. He is young, also." Her eyes bore into mine and I realized she might be stronger than I thought. "Can I give you a hug?"

Her question startled me a little; I wasn't usually touchy-feely outside of my immediate family unit. But I answered without hesitation. "Of course!"

She gripped me tight, and I sank into her embrace. I could feel her tremble and then shake. She was crying. As one, we stood in the hallway, swaying to our own heartbeats, until she whispered "thank you" in my ear and walked down the hall, away from the PICU. I felt lighter than I had in a while. I'd thought I was the one doing her the favor, giving the gift of touch and reassurance. I was mistaken. She had eased my load.

*****

12-2-06

You had a special visitor today! Santa came to see you; Ellie and Mikey were very bummed to have missed him.

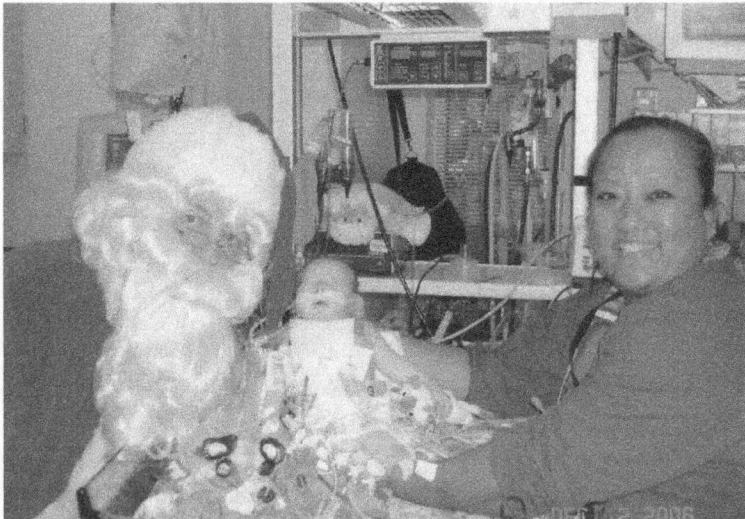

SANTA VISITS WITH CLINTON AND AN EXCEPTIONAL NURSE.

12-4-06

I got to hold you today!!! Your nurse overheard me say something to Poppy about how we haven't held you since the day of your surgery, and she said, "You are going to hold your son!" And she bundled you up, open chest, drugs, wires, tubes and all, and placed you in my arms. You cringed the whole way to me, which was hard to see, but you were fine once settled. I love you so much, My Little Man.

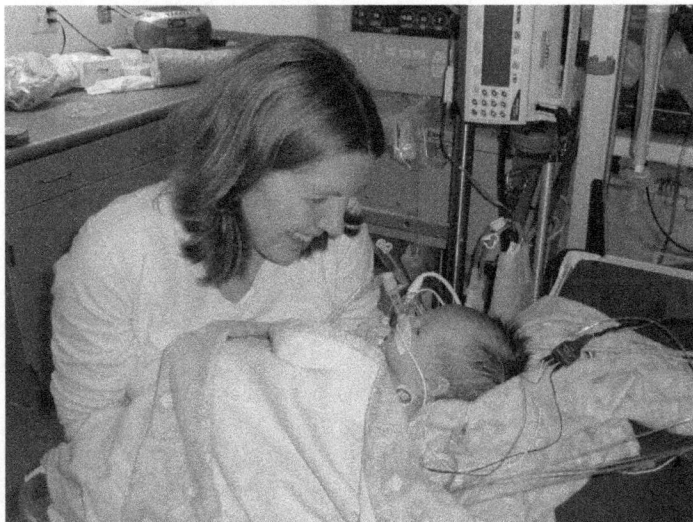

MOMMY GETS TO HOLD CLINTON FOR THE FIRST TIME SINCE SURGERY.

*****

CLINTON was quickly approaching million-dollar-baby status. And John's Family Leave and vacation hours were almost used up. We weren't sure if he could stay in Portland with us—and it was something we needed to figure out soon. Awesome insurance was keeping us afloat for the moment, but there had to be a cap at some point, plus non-medical expenses were stacking up.

As we stood in the hospital hallway, John's phone rang. It was his hospital, Kalispell Regional Medical Center. He'd only been on the job for about half a year, and now he'd been gone a month. Could they fire him? Would he have to go back to Montana?

John hung up.

"What? What was it?" I asked.

"That was work. They've all planned to pitch in hours from their Paid Time Off accounts and donate them to us. I can stay as long as we need."

*****

12-5-06

A BUSY COUPLE OF DAYS! Yesterday started well with you so alert and responsive, looking around and really seeing. Then they attempted to close your chest. After two to three hours, it was apparent that you weren't liking it, so they had to open you up again. They left in some sutures to keep you a little bit tighter in there than before.

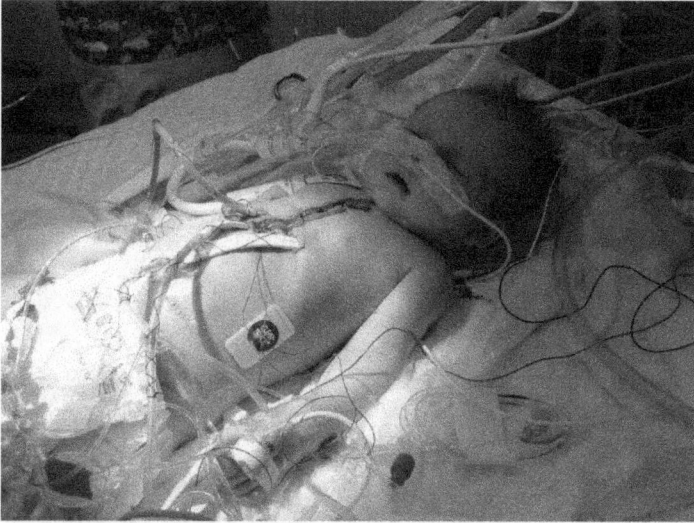

THE FIRST ATTEMPT AT CLOSING CLINTON'S CHEST LASTS ONLY A FEW HOURS.

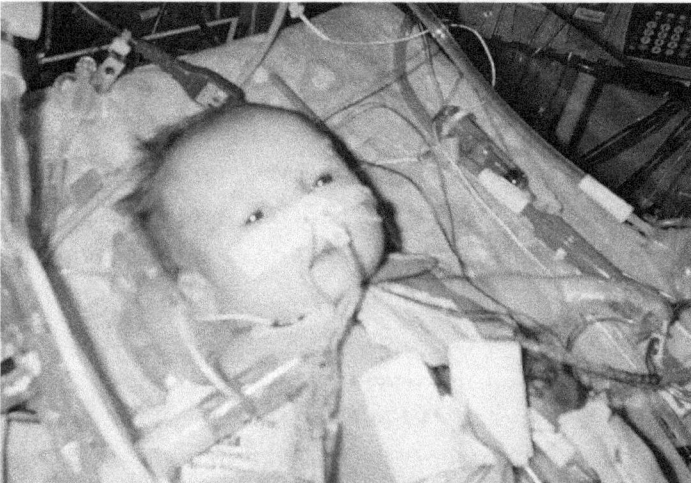

CLINTON AWAKE AND ALERT

You'd been smiling a lot, too, especially at Poppy's touch. This morning your PD catheter (for dialysis) started leaking a ton, so they had to hook you into a new catheter line through the subclavian/jugular region, and start running CVVH dialysis (blood circulation and cleansing rather than clear fluid exchange—a bit stronger and edgier for you and a new machine for your room). This type of dialysis is a lot more severe than PD. The initial ten minutes after hookup are the most crucial, as adding such a large blood volume at once to a little body can cause the blood pressure to plummet. You struggled, but then your pressures climbed and held somewhat steady.

It's been rocky since the machine was turned on, but you seem to be holding in there …. Please, Little Buddy—know that we love you and are thinking of you and NO MATTER WHAT, you are our Baby Boy. ALWAYS!

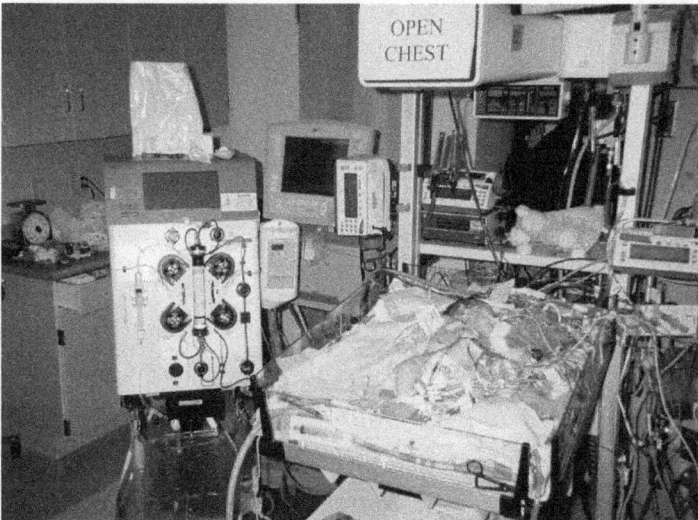

CLINTON ON DIALYSIS

12-5-06

WANTED TO NOTE that your main nurses have been absolutely wonderful, along with the doctors and residents. We have the best crew possible.

*****

THE plain card read: "Please feel free to write a note to baby Clinton and family." A Child-Life Specialist, whose job it is to help family members navigate the ups and downs of hospital life, left a journal for staff members to fill. As a teaching hospital, Doernbecher Children's Hospital/OHSU is filled with medical personnel who are learning on the job. Clinton had a major hand in forming the foundation of care on which these amazing people would be basing their entire career. We got to know them like an extended family; the Sullivans parading around the ward became a daily sight. Ellie and Mikey enjoyed walking the loop and waving to everyone they recognized. Several people took the time to leave entries for Clinton.

HANG in there big guy! Your family is the best around and you are stronger than the Energizer Bunny, Kiddo!

HEY Clinton! Hang in there big guy! We all love having your cute little face in here but we hope to see you get better soon.

SULLEY (you know, Sullivan), I know you give me the "stink eye" a lot, but I don't take it personally. I have much love for you, little friend. You are a lucky man and super blessed to have such an amazing mommy, daddy, Mikey, and Ellie who love you so much. Strength and peace.

TO my special boy Clinton and to his incredible family. You have touched my heart and soul to the core. You never cease to amaze me with your strength, compassion, and never-ending hope. My prayers are eternally with you. Stay strong. Love, the PICU nurse who will never stop working to help you get home.

CLINTON, you are a very special gift from your heavenly father to an awesome set of parents who are full of love and prayers for you and your siblings.

CLINTON, you are the most loved baby boy EVER! You and your family have an amazing strength. You keep us on our toes— continue to do that cuz we know it's your purpose in life to have lots of attention :) Stay sweet! Hugs little man, your transport to procedures friend.

*****

This Is Serious

Just Keep On Keeping On

12-6-06

ST. NICHOLAS! You got a book and a teether.

~*~

THIS MORNING the dialysis machine got clotted off and they had to turn it off at four a.m. When everyone in the medical crew arrived around ten a.m., they attempted to restart it and found out that you'd also clotted off your CVVH catheter. They ran echoes and x-rays and discovered you now have clots in the IJ and the subclavian (at the sight of the catheter). The heparin doesn't seem to be working, perhaps because it's been turned on and off.

We were called back to the hospital after our St. Nicholas festivities at home; one of your main doctors had been feeling concerned about you without being able to pinpoint why. That is how in tune she is with you. We had the kids come by before dinner, "just in case."

The reason came into fruition this evening. They decided to do a clot buster called a TPA—a very BIG and scary thing because it's strong enough to break up the clots, but can also dislodge a clot and send it through your system …. Watching them wrestle over the decision was intense; seeing such brilliant and caring people sitting there with their hands over their faces trying to go through the pros and cons of every choice ... but just before they could start it, you made a different decision for them. You started to hemorrhage from your nose and mouth.

So scary, Honey. And if they had given the TPA—I mean, they had no reason to know you were going to have such a blood issue before anything was even administered ....

We'd just gone to the cafeteria, and they had to call us over the hospital intercom to return to your room. I began shaking as soon as I heard our names; they had warned us to stay close. I squeezed Poppy's hand so tight as we walked back to your floor.

When we arrived, there were so many people trying to help you. Screens had been placed around the hallway to give as much privacy as possible, and there was not a dry eye in the area. Lots of love was going on. Unbelievably, almost everyone from the "main" crew was there, whether they'd been scheduled, just happened to be coming in for a meeting or to pick something up, or had been paged. Whatever the case, they all heard the call, and the circle of support was amazing.

Not only that, but the right specialists also "just happened" to be on hand; we didn't have to wait for anyone to be called to the hospital. You had all the help you needed!

As the doctors worked, a whole team of people was there doing whatever they could to help. Your main nurse was pushing blood and blood product in as fast as she could, while also manning the drugs and trying to keep her emotions at bay. Absolutely heart wrenching to watch. Amazing. The lead doctor and a GI specialist in particular were able to stop the bleeding by packing the back of your throat, but couldn't tell where the blood was coming from. They think perhaps it's an ulcer and that you have an infection—that you've gone septic.

You have so many drugs going on right now, and they're keeping you completely knocked out. You've started to pouf again. They ran a head scan and it's CLEAR!!! Everyone had been really concerned about a possible brain bleed. Mommy and Poppy were with you as soon as there was room at your bedside. We talked and sang, rubbed and held your hands and feet, cried, and tried to show you all of our love. The main crew all came by and cried and hugged and said prayers. A ring of doctors and nurses, all of different faiths, circled up and praying for you. Mind blowing. They are wonderful people.

12-7-06

YOU MADE IT through the night with vitals that are relatively stable. An IV line got clotted off. They're going to try a PICC line next. The plan is for you to try dialysis again; if your body can handle it, you'll be good. The fear is the necessary heparin (and bleeding risks because of it) due to your clotting issues. Also, your pressures are a bit low and you bottomed out last time they started dialysis when the pressures were higher and more stable. It would be nice if your pressures were higher before they tried. The doctors are really trying to come up with the best answer for you.

In the middle of all this is YOU, our sweet, precious, darling baby boy. This is heart, gut, and soul wrenching. We love you so much. We just ask for you to do what is right for you—to take your path and let us join you for as long as the journey takes. For you to be strong and do what you need to do. For us to be strong enough to follow your lead. You are amazing.

~*~

A NEW JOURNAL! This one was given to me by a Child-Life Specialist after the craziness on December 6th. You are again hooked up to dialysis. This time seems a bit smoother. You didn't drop your pressures too much or anything! Your poor abdomen is all purple and bruised (they took out your PD catheter because you have an infection in there, and because of all the heparin you're on, you bruise easily)—BUT you are still my sweet and oh-so-cute baby boy! I sing to you lots and rub your hair and feet. Poppy and I sang to you together for the first time today. I, of course, got all tearful.

You are almost a month old. Mikey turns two tomorrow. You kids are growing up so fast. Oh! Before the procedure today, your eyes were open and we got to really look at each other. I love you so much, my Little One. I forgot to write that Heidi (from Idaho) and her mother came to visit you a couple days ago! Very nice of them.

12-8-06

BABY, it's almost three in the morning and I am standing over your bassinet ... you are so beautiful and calm. I love standing so I can press my cheek or forehead against yours. I feel closer to you then, like we're actually snuggling and hugging.

Can you feel how much I love you? Earlier this evening, as I snuggled you and talked about you and life in general, you kept giving me half grins and trying to open your eyes. Sweet boy. Tonight was the first night I cried myself to sleep. I've been trying so hard to keep myself together and inside and NOT be so blubbery, but, by golly, right now you deserve some blubbering. You are an amazing boy and I so want to be able to bring you home. I miss your brother and sister a ton, too (we don't see them as often as usual, which for me—up until November—had been 24/7 ....)

Today, we will try to spend most of our time with them to celebrate Mikey's birthday and, sadly, it scares me to leave the hospital. Please hang in there, Little One, and hold strong! Today, you get more scans so we can see exactly where all your clots are and how they (and you) are doing. You do have an ulcer, I forgot to write. I love you forever!

*****

WE got to the apartment before Mikey woke up and tied two helium balloons to the back of his dining chair. A small chocolate cake was tucked in the fridge for later. Mikey and Ellie spent a good portion of the day running across the living room, with the new two-year-old slowing down only to check if the balloon was following him. We ate breakfast at a restaurant and then brought a huge Costco sheet cake to the PICU staffroom for everyone to enjoy. Finding special moments to celebrate was important for everyone. Any way to make life feel normal and balanced made it easier for us to stand steady during the moments when the world shook.

One nurse brought a gift of gummy worms and a balloon for him. "How old are you today, buddy?"

"Two!"

And for several days afterward, that was his answer to everything.

LEAVING THE HOSPITAL TO CELEBRATE A BIRTHDAY BOY

HAPPY SECOND BIRTHDAY, MIKEY!
*****

12-10-06

ONE MONTH OLD!!! Oh, Sweetie, you have come so far, been through so much. You amaze me. So strong, so young …. Today, you spontaneously smiled at me in response to my smiles to you! When you're alert, your dark eyes are huge and look around everywhere. You are so endearing and have just an amazing spark about you.

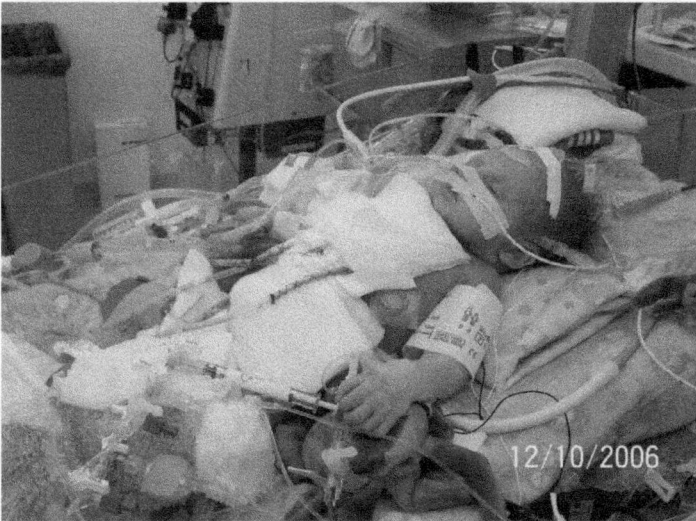

A ONE-MONTH BIRTHDAY BOY

People literally all across the United States are loving you, praying for you, and thinking of you. You have connected so many people in their love for you (like that awful night of hemorrhaging a few days ago—I've never seen or felt a room so full of love and support—all for YOU!) What a special Little One, and what a unique role you have.

Honey, you mean so much to us, and we just ache to hold and cuddle you. We saw your tushie and backside for the first time today when we helped with your bath (you've been on your back since birth). Now that you are "shrunk," you are so small (no fat on you yet, though you have very cute jowly cheeks!), with very long fingers and toes. I think you measure about twenty-one to twenty-two inches! Amazing how you keep growing even as your body goes through all of this craziness.

Sweetie, thank you so much for being in our lives. We are blessed to have you. No matter what, you are a huge and loved part of our family and we are completely thankful that you came to our family! I hope we can be as strong for you as you have been for us. We love you ALWAYS. Happy one-month birthday!

12-11-06

A *BIG* DAY FOR YOU! Your chest was closed today and it looks like, this time, it will stay that way! Your skin, however, is still mostly open. It's too fragile to suture, so they'll work on that later, or see if it will heal on its own. Also, you may be having issues with your kidneys. But, overall, a good day. We love you kiddo. So much. Forever and ever.

12-12-06

ANOTHER DAY OF MILESTONES! It started a bit on the down side, because you were still bleeding from your surgery site. They turned off your heparin to see if your chest would stop the ooze, but it had no effect. The surgeons came in to make sure they wouldn't have to open you again, and they ended up cauterizing and packing the wound and it's doing much better. You are amazing. We love you.

*****

WE purchased a Christmas tree to decorate with ornaments donated to us by the hospital. Gorgeous origami stars, silly Disney characters, Hallmark figures .... Things were so rocky with Clinton, the whole time we were at the tree lot, we jumped whenever John's phone rang. We dreaded getting a call from the hospital.

*****

12-13-06

DIALYSIS DIDN'T WORK AGAIN, with the same issues as last time—clotting up and everything. They're trying again tomorrow. Be strong, Little One. We love you SO MUCH, darling.

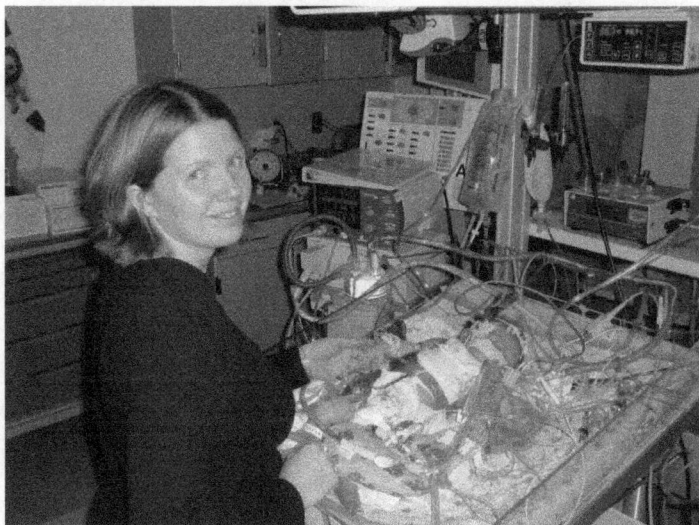

A VERY SICK LITTLE BOY

12-14-06

YOU'RE ON DIALYSIS, Sweetie. Will it work? Oh, please, Honey. Do whatever is right for you. You had some crying times today—so hard to see, but then you can be totally comforted by us. You open your hands before you cry, as if you're asking for us, and then we put our fingers into your palm. You grip hard and stop crying! Once, when it was just me holding your right hand, you continued to cry a bit, so I called Poppy over and said you needed him. As soon as you gripped his finger too, you calmed down. Also, I can rub your head and press my forehead against yours and sing, and you will be soothed. So sweet. We love you. Your eyes, which are losing their newborn slate gray color, search back and forth between us. We see you, Honey. We are here for you, and we will always love you.

Letting Go

12-15-06
You died today, Honey, at 6:20 a.m.

My Other Heart

A Letter to John

12-16-06

Dear Baby-doll,

Sweetie, you mean so much to me. Thank you for your strength, love, and support during this past month. You are such a wonderful person, husband, and Poppy. Little Clinton loved you so much, Honey. I could tell by the way his eyes searched for you, the way his hand reached for you, the way he gripped your finger; you could get him to smile and fan his toes by rubbing his tiny feet. You were able to comfort, cuddle, kiss, and caress your little son. He could tell that he was loved by you and was able to be calmed by your touch.

This has been an insane time for us. It is our love for our wee son, our family, and each other that has gotten us through this far and will continue to help us pass each day.

Clinton was such a special baby, so full of life and love. We will miss him very much, always, but it won't always be so painful. Thank you for holding me, loving me, and letting me cry. I support and love you very much. I am so thankful for the time we

had with Clinton and as a family of five. Forever and ever, Honey.
No matter what.

Love, me

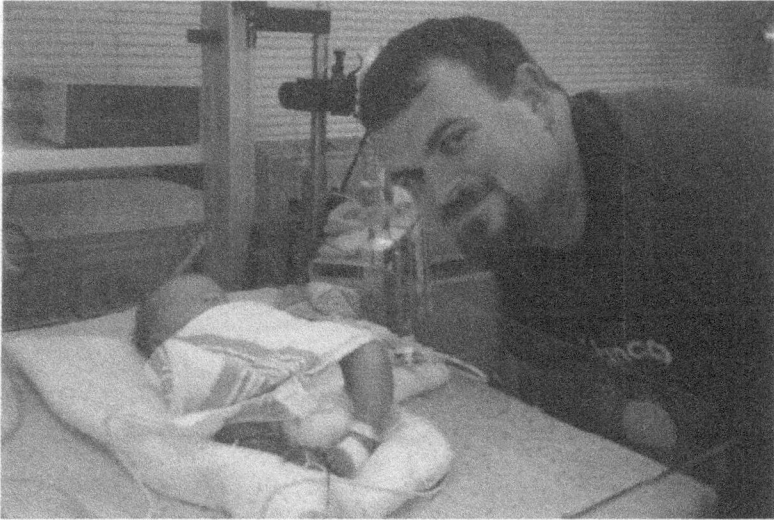

REMEMBERING LIFE

Looking Back to December 15

Life Is Death; Death Is Life

A massive windstorm blew through the Portland area on the evening of the 14th. Normally, I slept alone at the hospital. But the wind was positively howling, and the air felt heavy and dark. Concerned about a potential power outage, John decided to stay the night with me. He wanted to be on hand if there were any issues with the backup generators. Clinton's various machines required electricity. Because of his decision, John was with me the morning of the 15th. Otherwise, I would have been alone.

*****

12-17-06

IT HAS TAKEN ME some time to get back to your journal ….

December 15th was the hardest and most abstractly amazing day I have ever experienced. Poppy woke up shortly before six a.m. and heard you beeping strangely. He went to you and held your hand, while the nurse was bag suctioning you. He saw your pressures plummet and came to wake me up.

By the time I walked around your bedside, the room was already filling with people. Poppy and I moved to just outside your doorway. There was a lot of asking what should be done, who should be called in, etc; all the while, a flurry of drugs and machine and manual intervention was occurring. They hooked up both sides of your pacers with no effect and three to four people took turns with chest compressions. At one point, the doctor stepped out and told us, "You guys, I don't think he can make it through this one." Everyone was so used to pulling you from the brink.

A bit later, one of the nurses asked us if we wanted to come up to your bedside. Of course we did! They were still trying chest compressions as we kissed your forehead and stroked your arms. There was a quick pause and someone asked, "What should we try now?"

And I looked away from your beautiful face and said, "We would like to hold him."

The room grew quiet like a deep sigh and seemed to take a step back from your little body, and with a slow breath, the room moved again and the nurses began to unplug everything. They wrapped you up in your blanket and handed you to me. Poppy and I fell together with you in-between us and we just held each other.

People came and went. We began to make phone calls, Grandma Betsy first, and she said she'd bring over the kids. One of the residents and your first nurse in the PICU were with us. The charge nurse for the day came in and out. Everyone wanted to hold you and share their love and sadness with us. Even your main doctor, who had the day off, came by.

When Mikey and Ellie showed up, we took them into a separate room and told them your heart had stopped working and you wouldn't be able to come home with us. We were quiet and let Ellie's questions guide us. Ellie said she wanted to see you, and Mikey said yes, too, so we went to your room. Ellie then said she wanted to hold you. She sat in a rocking chair; you lay on her lap with me supporting you. She whispered to you, making sure you'd remember her and things from your life here. She went to play on the bed behind yours for a bit, but then came back and wanted to hold you again. She took off your hat and rubbed your soft sweet hair, caressed your little face, and gently opened your beautiful eyes. Bending forward, she looked closely at you and stated she wanted you to remember her, because you weren't going to be with us anymore. She loves you, we *all* do, so very much; it's hard to say goodbye.

Ellie cuddled you for a very long time. Mikey rubbed your head and watched you silently before he went off to play quietly. A resident who also had the day off stayed with the kiddos and kept them occupied as we dealt with everything.

The children left and we held you and cried and smiled and loved you. We talked to the surgeons about an autopsy and decided if they felt they could learn from you (as everyone had while you were living), then they could perform their procedure. They thought you'd be very helpful and will put your heart in their archives for future students to learn from as well. Clinton, you were always a teacher in so many ways. So many people told us how touched and changed they were because of *you*, a wee one, just five weeks old. You are amazing. And beautiful. You take my breath away.

We talked to a Hospital Director and got the name of a crematorium. We took your photo, took hand and foot prints, and made a plaque of your hand …. Then it was time.

We were able to take you, with two of your day nurses, on your last physical journey, your last parade through the hospital, down to the morgue. I handed you over to a third nurse, and we said a final goodbye to your body. So sweet and small. Honey, we love you so much and miss you so much already. What an amazing boy.

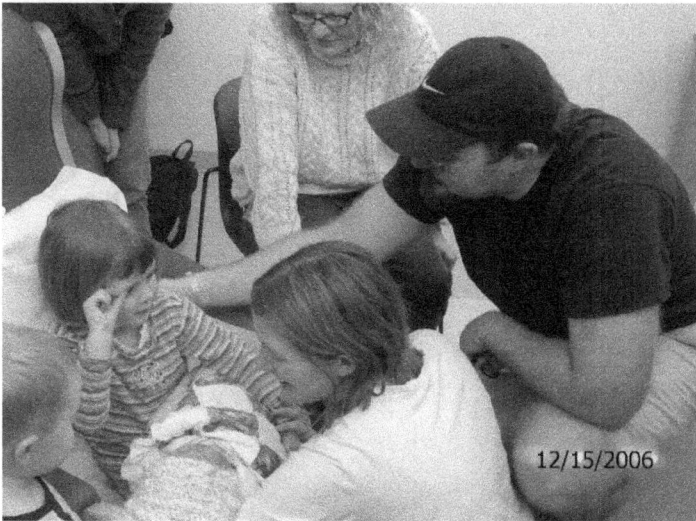

LETTING GO WITH OUR HANDS BUT NOT OUR HEARTS
*****

CLINTON died on the very last day Grandma Betsy could stay with us. We had plans for a friend to come out the next morning to care for the children; instead, we'd be driving home.

"Oh, Hannah!" Amy's shattered voice came over the line. "I am so, so sorry." She paused to compose herself. "I can't even imagine ...."

"Don't," I said. "Don't imagine. You don't want to. Go hug and kiss your girls. Love them up for me."

"I was all ready to fly out tomorrow morning. Everything is packed ...."

"I know."

"I'm so sorry."

"I know."

I shared a lot of love and thoughts and feelings that day. What surprised me the most was the protective feeling I had towards other people; I wanted to make them feel better about everything, see that it was a day of love, ease their sorrow. I suppose I didn't want the thought of Clinton to cause anyone pain. Even on our

93

walk to the morgue, I carried Clinton wrapped in his blanket and avoided eye contact with people in the halls. Not because of how I felt, but because I didn't want to startle them with the image of a newborn, only for them to realize that it wasn't a celebratory walk we were taking.

*****

On December 16th, I woke up with absolutely no idea where I was. The room was dark, the bed big, soft, and white. It was facing the wrong way; I wasn't at home. And it was quiet. Too quiet. I jerked upright. The hospital. Clinton. Then it sank in: I was at the apartment. I hadn't ever slept there before.

Grandma Betsy was starting to pack our things, the children assisting by climbing into empty laundry baskets and searching through totes for toys. John came into the bedroom to help me unwind my bindings. Unfortunately, when your baby dies, your body doesn't get the memo. My chest, so sore from the excess of milk, made it impossible for me to lift my arms or reach around to undo the bandage on my own.

I kissed my husband and headed to the bathroom connected to our room. Turning on the shower, I stepped into the warmth, and bawled. Somehow, through the noise of the fan and the rush of water, John heard me—because there he was, opening the door and pulling me to him. While I let it all go, he held me together.

*****

12-18-06

WE HAD THE CREMATION PERFORMED by Autumn (perfectly named for the season in which you were born), and picked up your ashes today before heading out of town (towards Idaho to visit friends and share the memory of you). So odd to be picking you up in a cute white ceramic box. So odd to be driving away from Portland, away from our home at the hospital, away from the people who knew you as well as, if not better than, we did .... So strange to not have you. You were little—yet hugely strong. We will continue your strength for you. We will love and remember you. We will be better because of you. Thank you for being in our lives, for touching us so deeply, for bringing such a great love into our existence. You are a miracle.

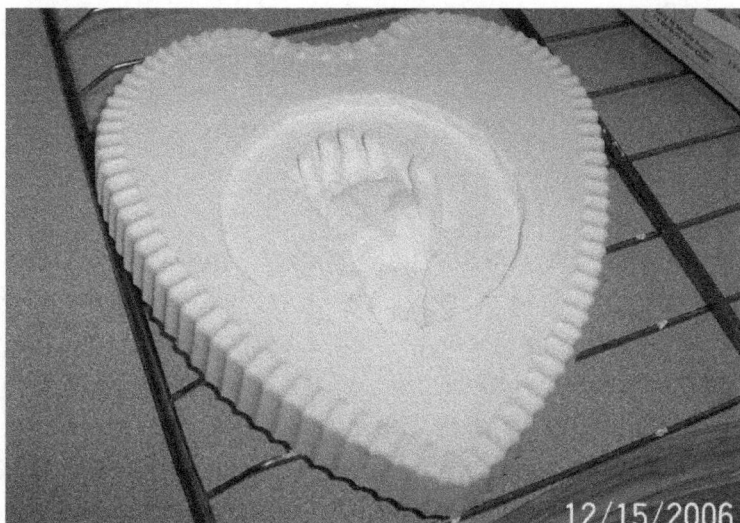

CLINTON'S HAND PLAQUE

A New Normal

The Happiness Within

WHO would have thought the lack of dust could ever be a sign of love and comfort? It may seem silly in the whole scheme of things after what we'd gone through, but I was secretly dreading the arrival to our house, where things like dusty wooden floors and shelves would await. It didn't seem right to come home after six weeks of emotional overload and be faced with mundane chores. Only, when we got home and I began to clean, there was no dust. Not one speck.

Returning to our lives was something best done by jumping in with our eyes and hearts wide open. People knew I had been pregnant and they wanted to know how our Little One was. It was a judgement call with each person, how to phrase it, how much to say, how honest to be. Not everyone had known about the heart issues to begin with. So I'd hold my chin up, take a breath, and say what came. And try to make it as gentle as possible because, no matter how I said it, it was a shock for people to hear.

"Oh, we had a sweet baby boy. He had to have surgery after birth and ended up having complications. He died a little before Christmas."

People shared hugs and gave me the gift of their own tears. Being honest brought strength and healing, and usually struck a chord with whomever I was talking. It was surprising how many people had their own stories; Clinton's tale could open floodgates. There was a secret club out there of people who shared a life of Before and After. Many didn't feel they could talk about it; many didn't know how.

*****

From: JohnandHannah@email.com
To: Krista@email.com
Sent: Friday, December 29, 2006
Subject: Attitude

Hey there!
I got this from my mother-in-law today and thought I'd forward it to you. It's perfect.

ATTITUDE
There once was a woman who woke up in the morning, looked in the mirror, and noticed she had only three hairs on her head. "Well," she said, "I think I will braid my hair today." So she did, and she had a wonderful day.

The next day she woke up, looked in the mirror, and saw that she had only two hairs on her head. "Hmm," she said, "I think I'll part my hair down the middle today." So she did, and she had a grand day.

The next day she woke up, looked in the mirror, and noticed that she had only one hair on her head. "Well," she said, "today I'm going to wear my hair in a ponytail." So she did, and she had a fun day.

The next day she woke up, looked in the mirror, and noticed that there wasn't a single hair on her head. "Yea!" she exclaimed, "I don't have to fix my hair today!"

Attitude is everything. Be kinder than necessary, for everyone you meet is fighting some kind of battle.

Isn't that lovely? It is so, so true; life is all about being able to shift your perspective. Have a gorgeous day!
Love, Hannah

~~~

From: BetsyS@email.com
To: JohnandHannah@email.com
Sent: Saturday, December 30, 2006
Subject: hi my family

I post almost daily to an online support group that is actually for weight loss. But we all share our family and personal issues as well. They were all praying for Clinton during his lifetime. I wanted to share one post with you from a friend in Maryland:

"Betsy: I am glad to hear your family is holding up well during this difficult time of the death of baby Clinton. It sounds like you are all doing such wonderful things to show him your love and to honor his time with you.

When little ones are here for such a short time it is sometimes hard to imagine they could achieve their life's purpose ... that everything could be accomplished that should be.

I believe they are. Look at all the lives he touched all over the country in our little group. He brought a lot of love with him and passed it around. It's just what our world needs. He's watching over all of us. Thank you, Baby Clinton. Thank you, Betsy, for sharing him with us."

While this post makes me tear up, it is also a wonderful thought. Hope you guys are doing okay.

Love from Mom/Grandma B

*****

Our whole take on life and death changed. For us, it was just a normal part of our lives. Outsiders might feel it was morbid; our family incorporated it into our daily activities.

Ellie carried her swaddled baby doll to me, asking, "You wanna hold her?"

"Sure," I answered, reaching for the toy.

With a dramatically mournful voice, Ellie continued. "She's already dead. They haven't had her cremation yet."

When Mikey was a little older, after eating a meal he found particularly yummy, he exclaimed, "Mmm, I'm dead!"

It took me a moment to realize he was using my phrase of ultimate bliss: "Oh, I'm in heaven!"

*****

From: JohnandHannah@email.com
To: Krista@email.com
Sent: Saturday, January 1, 2007
Subject: hi

Hello there! So funny that you mentioned writing Clinton's story .... After he died, on our looooong way home, John mentioned that he wanted to type up the journal I'd kept for the wee one, and I'd been thinking the same thing. To share with friends and family so they can get a glimmer of Clinton ... several people have told me I should publish it. I wouldn't know how to get that done, but I think it would be so cool for Clinton to go on teaching people, helping, and healing. What a legacy .... Perhaps someday, something will happen. Until then, at some point we will print copies of his journal and give them to people who want his (and our) story ....

It was great talking with you the other day. I hope you all are super, that Christmas was magical, and that your New Year will be filled with love!

Oh! I forgot to tell you about my present from John: He'd been looking for ID bracelets for us (to put Clinton's name and birthdate down in something permanent to wear instead of our hospital bracelets), and on a whim, at the last place he went to, he also asked if they carried birthstone rings. The lady said yes and showed him the case. John looked for the November rings, and there, in the center of the case, was one. Heart shaped. Set in white gold, the only color I wear, with two individual stones set on either side. He bought it without batting an eye; he knew it was there for me.

He also got me a little container made by the Willow Tree company (the figurines I collect). On the cover is a little boy holding a golden heart; on the inside is the quote: "You will always have my heart." Ah, my little Clinton Jacob .... For me that is what he will always represent. Love. Love and teaching. What a wonderful combo, and what an amazing Little Guy.

Love, Hannah

~~~

From: JohnandHannah@email.com
To: Krista@email.com
Sent: Wednesday, January 17, 2007
Subject: Thanks

Hi Krista! Just thinking about you and wanted to say hi and I love you. I'm really missing Clinton today, so it meant a ton when I went down to the mailbox and there was a card from Shannon. Could you tell her it meant so much to me? Thank you for sharing our boy with her. :-) As soon as I figure out how to do pictures on our laptop, I'll send some out to you.

Best wishes to all, Hannah

~~~

From: JohnandHannah@email.com
To: Krista@email.com
Sent: Tuesday, February 6, 2007
Subject: Hi (long!)

Hi Krista! I'm so glad you got the CD ... I'm thinking if it's not working, it's probably the one I tried to burn (John made the others), so I must have done it wrong ... oops! We'll burn another (we've got a bunch more to make) and send it to you soon.

There are a couple stories behind the songs .... All of the songs, as John wrote on the back of the CD case, remind us of Clinton and our time with him. First of all, the Norah Jones songs came from the hospital—we played that CD a lot in Clinton's room. It was playing when he died, too, and the nurse said we just had to take it home with us. The Sarah Evans music was what we listened to on all our back-and-forthing to the hospital. When I was alone in the car, I'd roll down the windows and blast it!

Now, another CD that played a lot at the hospital was one by Sarah McLachlan. Hers was on the night of the hemorrhaging .... While everything was happening that night, and we thought we were going to lose him then, I told John, "If anything happens, I want to play that angel song at whatever service we have." When he died several days later, the resident that we loved so much came in on her day off and sat with us that whole day (one of our favorite nurses did, too) and played with the kids while John and I were busy with "stuff." When we got home, we couldn't find our copy of the angel CD anywhere, and I desperately wanted it. While Christmas shopping, I was able to find ONE copy of it—and only at one store—but I decided not to buy it in case John was getting it for me. He actually was looking for it, but could not find any copies. The day after his failed search, we received a package from ... our favorite resident. The gift inside was the angel CD. She wrote that the angel song played on her car radio as she drove away from the hospital after leaving us that day, and she knew she had to get the CD for us ....

While coming up with the list of songs I wanted to include on Clinton's memorial CD, I knew there was a Sarah Evans song that had struck me as special and powerful, but didn't know the song title, the words that had been meaningful, or which of her CDs it was on. I chose another song in its place, got the kids together, and hopped in the car to go grocery shopping. As the car started, THE song came on at THE exact phrase that meant so much to me. It's the "Rocking Horse" one on your CD. Listen to that one closely; I call it our theme song (the "If You're Going Through Hell" song by Rodney Atkins is another of our themes).

At the same time the kids and I were getting groceries, John was at Target looking for John Lennon's song. He couldn't find Lennon anywhere, so he gave up and went to the country section to look for some other music. Something caught the corner of his eye. He turned to look. John Lennon's Greatest Hits. One copy. Sitting right there with the good ol' country stuff. Song number fourteen? THE song.

All I can say is: "Thank you, thank you, thank you!!!!!" Isn't life beautiful?

The drawing on the cover is one I made when I was sixteen. Sixteen!!! Why would I draw an angel carrying a baby? It's the only baby thing I have ever drawn, too. The picture on the CD itself was taken in December of last year, the range has the peak on which we plan to scatter Clinton's ashes. The poem came from a friend who lost her twins when she went into premature labor. The words are perfect, exactly how we feel. John put everything together and wrote the message on the back. It's our little work of love for our sweet little boy. When you listen to it, I hope you get a feel for him. I love you so much.

Love, Hannah

~~~

From: BetsyS@email.com
To: JohnandHannah@email.com
Sent: Friday, February 16, 2007
Subject: Good Morning

Hi my family. I realized last night that yesterday was the two-month anniversary of dear Clinton's death. I want you to know that I remember him and love him every day. I had a sad, sad time again last night and was just feeling bad for the little guy. But, today is a new day and I remember that he was sent to us to show us the power of love, strength, and courage. He also showed us how important family and friends are.

Loving you all, Mom/Grandma

*****

"CINTON!" Mikey yelled. "Bup, bup. See Cinton!"

Back in January, he had begun to refer to his little brother simply as "baby." But he had just seen a new photo of Clinton on the fridge.

I scooped him up so he could get a closer look, and he immediately bent forward to give the image pats and kisses. Squirming out of my arms, he yelled again. "Cinton!"

"What is it, Sweetie?" I couldn't understand what he was trying to tell me and now he was getting frustrated and pointing out of the room.

"See Cinton, see!"

"Show me, Honey." Taking my hand, he led me down the hall and into the master bedroom.

Pointing up to the plaster cast of Clinton's hand hanging on our wall, Mikey said, "Look, see!" So I picked him up again, and he gently touched it. Afterwards, he took me to the hallway where family photos lined the walls. He wanted to look at each of Clinton's. It was like he had the need to remember. From that point on, I had us give shouts out to Clinton whenever we had the urge. Randomly we'd holler, "Clinton, I love you!" or anything we wanted to put out there.

Mikey liked sharing brotherly information, like: "Cinton! I have goosebumps on mine hieney!"

On March 12th, Mikey had something else to say while I was lying on the couch. He patted my belly, and then rested his head on it. "Bay-bee."

A week later we understood why.

*****

From: JohnandHannah@email.com
To: Krista@email.com
Sent: Thursday, March 15, 2007
Subject: Hi!

Hey Krista! My sister Sarah had her baby girl today; she doesn't have a first name yet (!), but her middle name is Claire. I think that's pretty. She says the baby is chubby and fair-haired. I go out to visit at the end of April. I'm so happy for them, but it gets me yearning for a little one. Ah, well …. One day!

It's weird having three kids, but only *having* two. When I get asked how many I have or how old they are, or people say "they're really close together; you must have your hands full!" I want to say, "Wait! I have another. His name is Clinton. He died when he was five weeks old, but he was close in age, too. I don't have my hands full; they're a third empty. It's my heart that's full. And I want more …." But I smile and answer, and sometimes I say

"I've had three babies so far," and if it's the right time, I'll tell them about Clinton. I do love sharing him. Thanks for the ear!
    Love, Hannah

*****

CLINTON'S death had felt like two losses for me: the loss of Clinton, himself, and the loss of a newborn baby. Clinton could never be replaced; I would keep him just as he was—in my heart forever. But a new baby would give us all the opportunity to experience the continuation of life. Hopefully in a very mellow, very typical fashion. I wanted the kids to be able to live and grow with a younger sibling, and my arms ached to hold a small bundle of baby-love. I also wanted to hear that soft, whiffley breathing and rub my cheek against a downy little head.

    We'd been told to wait a year. Oops. Our "year" was only a few months .... I guess I never did get the patience I'd so been wanting! Ah, well—I'd rather have a baby, anyway.

*****

Beginning Again

The Light Keeps Spreading

ELLIE, darling girl, was full of big thoughts when we told her our news. "Mommy! Maybe Clinton picked out this baby so we could love it because Clinton can't be here with us." We were due a week after Clinton's first birthday.

*****

AT the end of April, I visited Sarah in California, to meet her daughter, Lana Claire. On the flight home, I was seated next to a middle-aged woman who looked heartbroken. When I heard her sniff, I could no longer remain an outsider. Turning to her, I asked, "Are you okay?" I mean, obviously she wasn't, but how do you start conversations like that with a stranger? It was all the prompting she needed, though.

"No. I've just come from my grandson's funeral, and I'm so sad and I don't know what to do."

Well. A conversation made just for the two of us. We could have been placed anywhere on the plane, next to anyone. Instead, we were given each other. Thanks to Clinton, long gone were my days of little physical contact with people outside my personal safety zone. When she gripped my hand, I held onto hers. For the entire flight back home.

*****

105

From: JohnandHannah@email.com
To: Krista@email.com
Sent: Monday, June 11, 2007
Subject: Howdy

Hi there! Just wanted to let you know that this Thursday we're driving to Missoula (about two hours away) to meet with the heart specialist for a fetal heart cardiogram .... This appointment should let us know what we can expect with this wee one! So hope everything is good; our regular ultrasound is scheduled for July 5th, just before Clinton's memorial. Cannot wait to see this baby!!!!! Looking forward to the memorial, too—it's going to be a bit of a reunion, and we'll be planting some trees with Clinton's ashes.

    Love, Hannah

~~~

From: JohnandHannah@email.com
To: Krista@email.com
Sent: Wednesday, June 13, 2007
Subject: Hi

Hi there! I so hope everything goes well for your sister's family. I have a friend whose youngest had a cancer that required him to be in and out of the hospital for the first couple years of his life. He's six now and is totally okay. I can't imagine the stress and fear. I really wish them well—lots of strength and peace and love.

    There was a saying in the PICU about how parents were always thankful for what their child had: "Oh, thank goodness, it's just his heart" or "Thank goodness it's only cancer" or "Thank goodness it's this and not that ...." And we'd all look at each other and wonder, "Wow, how can they handle that?" It must be some kind of defense mechanism. It's all HUGE, if you know what I mean. Isn't that odd?

    This appointment tomorrow is to take a thorough look at the baby's heart. There is a low chance (3-5%) of reoccurrence, though it's not hereditary. Something like 1 in 110 kids are born with some form of heart issue (small or large; able to heal on its own or not). It's one of the most common congenital "defects" (oooh, I cannot stand that word). Clinton's problem was not as common as that, hence the trip to Portland. So, it's a low chance, but possible. (Clinton had a 95-99% chance of making it, after all!) They want us to be prepared for anything. We're not going to find out the sex; we like the surprise. I'll let you know what we learn.

It sounds like you are all as busy as usual; I love that your kids are into sports and activities. So good and healthy.

Take care of yourself and hugs all around.

Love, Hannah

~~~

From: JohnandHannah@email.com
To: Krista@email.com
Sent: Sunday, June 17, 2007
Subject: hi

Hey Krista! How are you? Just wanted to let you know the echo looked good!!!! Because the baby's so young now (17-18 weeks), they want another echocardiogram in a month (July 12th) and, just for good measure, they'll run one on the baby when he/she is born. The doctor sounds really pleased, which is good. With Clinton, it was in July that his heart issue was suspected, and then our following appointment in August confirmed it.

Did I tell you the baby's due date is just a couple days off from Clinton's birthdate? Very interesting to have such a duplicate in pregnancy milestones and stages. I'm just starting to feel him/her shift around in there and make little "plip" feelings. So exciting!

All the best, Hannah

*****

I was completely in love with this little one. I wasn't counting on the tests to alleviate all the buried worries; I don't think parents ever stop worrying about their children. But, I felt that if something were to go a bit sideways, we'd be able to handle it. The baby I'd miscarried before becoming pregnant with Clinton had shown me I could love something and say goodbye without cracking. Clinton had shown me I could love a child so much that letting him go wouldn't shatter me absolutely. Maybe they somehow knew John and I could be strong enough for them to live out their lives, no matter what direction their lives took.

But I really hoped this baby was here to teach us about how to live a very, very long and fruitful life.

*****

From: JohnandHannah@email.com
To: Krista@email.com
Sent: Thursday, June 28, 2007
Subject: Hi!

Today, we went on a hike up that mountain on your CD cover. We got only halfway (you drive about halfway up the mountain and then it's about a three-mile hike to the peak), because of the time, but we got to a beautiful ridge and scattered some of Clinton's ashes there. When we go next, we'll bring him all the way up to the peak.

For the memorial on the 7th, we're going to scatter some ashes under four crabapple trees we'll plant in the yard—one in each corner around the play structure. It cracks me up because Ellie calls it "planting Clinton"! He still makes me smile. We carried "him" in a snack cup today and joked that he was just like Ellie and Mikey, who got to ride in back-pack carriers. Oh, you! ;-)

How are you? When's your trip to California? I hope you have bunches of fun.

Love, Hannah

*****

"HANNAH?"

"Yeah?"

"I have something to share with you ...."

"Ooo-kaay. What's up?" My sister's excited voice held a note that I didn't recognize and I was completely curious.

"Well, I was having a really hard day today, thinking about Clinton and just feeling so sad. We had his music on and Lana and I danced to it, just spinning and thinking. You know?"

"Yeah, I know." I smiled into my phone at the image. Sweet three-month-old Lana had shown ties to her cousin already; one of her first bubbling and cooing moments was while looking at Clinton's photo on their fridge.

"So we were just out driving—Scott was sleeping in the front seat and Lucas was playing in his car seat. And ..." Her voice lilts. "... I looked out my side window. There was a van there. Like a moving van or delivery van or something ...."

"Yeah?"

"There was a sign on its side. And, Hannah, it said: "Rest in peace Clinton."

*****

THE *memorial on July 7th was perfect, though insanely hot. Inside our house, we'd set up a table with hospital memorabilia, Clinton's journal, books on grief, and the scrapbook I'd made with cards we'd received. Outside, Clinton's music played in the background as we took turns talking about him. Afterwards, everyone scattered his ashes in the four holes we'd dug for the crabapple trees around the children's play structure. The ropes securing the burlap sacks over the root balls formed perfect stars.*

Ellie took the pinch of her ashes into the actual sand box, so he could be with her when she played. Sprinkling sand on top, she stated, "I'm burying him now." A pause while she added even more sand on top. "And I'm burying him again!" Ever the concerned big sister, if brother Mikey or cousin Lucas stood too close to her pile, she'd shout, "You're standing on Clinton! I need SPACE!"

*****

From: JohnandHannah@email.com
To: Karen@email.com
Sent: Saturday, September 28, 2007
Subject: Hi!

Hey there, Karen! It was great talking to you. I'm so glad you can send the website link!!! I still can't believe that my heart and footprint pendant disappeared from the chain. But … I had a miracle of sorts occur at the end of the day it was lost, after I called you. I was walking down the steps inside our garage and something fell on my foot. I looked down, and there was my heart, hours later and after a nap! I'd already shaken out my shirt and everything. Pretty cool, huh?! So, I'd love to have the link on hand, just in case the pendant disappears again. I may even order it now to make sure I have backup! It means that much to me; it was the perfect gift. I hope you are doing super–well! I'll write or call soon.

Love ya! Hannah

*****

ELLIE *was thoughtful when I picked her up from her half-day of preschool. "How was your day, Sweetie? Did you have fun on your fieldtrip?"*

"We didn't go on it today."

"No? What a bummer. Why not?"

"'Cause the bus driver died."

"The bus driver? What happened?" In my head I was thinking, Oh my gosh. Today? With you kids?

"Yup, he was gonna take us, but he couldn't come 'cause he died."

"Um, when?" Are you supposed to interrogate your kid to get answers for something like this? Probably not, but Ellie seemed composed enough. And we were completely open in our family about things like death.

"On the weekend."

Whew. "Oh, that's too bad. How do you feel about it?"

"Fine. He was old. And he's in heaven with Clinton!" Well, she sure did sound okay. "Does he have his bus there?"

"Ha! I bet he does, Honey. Maybe he's up there driving Clinton around and giving him a grand tour of the place. What do you think?"

"Oh, yes mommy! They'd have fun!"

110

*****

From: JohnandHannah@email.com
To: Karen@email.com
Sent: Thursday, October 3, 2007
Re: Hi!

Hey Karen! I am so sorry to hear about your father's diagnosis. That must have been difficult for everyone to adjust to. How is everyone doing? Sounds like it was a fun trip, and I know you will cherish every one of those memories. I love that you are a close family. Sooooo important, that family strength. Thanks for the photo; it's such a sweet picture. The glaciers must have been breathtaking. I've heard that sometimes they look like they're glowing from the inside. Magical! You'll all be in our thoughts!

    Love, Hannah

~~~

From: BetsyS@email.com
To: JohnandHannah@email.com
Sent: Saturday, October 27, 2007
Subject: Lyrics to Kenny Chesney song

Hi. Ok, so I downloaded the song you were talking about—Who You'd Be Someday— and keep playing it! Thought I'd send you the lyrics. It is a great song and makes me cry again for our baby. And my mind is totally back in Portland! The trees, the wet streets, the rain, Multnomah, Terwilliger, Fred Meyer, park, dog park, leaves, cold, the rain, driving kids around, the zoo, the apartment, the shopping center, taking the kids to Target, the rain. And of course, our dear baby Clinton, the hospital, the nurses, the joys, the sadness, the loss. Makes me sad.

    Love you! Mom/Grandma

~~~

From: JohnandHannah@email.com
To: BetsyS@email.com
Sent: Saturday, October 27, 2007
Re: Lyrics to Kenny Chesney song

Oh goodness. Now I'm gonna be teary, too, reading those words. I'm with you and your remembrances. I can so picture/feel/remember everything …. I can focus on a certain spot in the hospital and remember the emotions connected to that specific room/space/hallway. I can remember the constant feelings of joy, hope, sadness, and aching. The constant up-and-downing. Being so tired, down to my core, and not even realizing I was asleep until I was waking up. Of dreading making "that" phone call to John. Praying that if anything happened, that Clinton could just hold on until we were there. Of missing the kids sooooo much. Of just wanting to hold my boy. The smell of his hair, his jowly cheek, the clasp of his hand.

There are times that Mikey feels or looks so much like him …. I remember the day Clinton died and John and I were walking to the car and Norah Jones's song "The Long Day is Over" came into my head, and that is just how I felt.

We had every kind of weather that afternoon. Sunshine breaking through the clouds as we carried his wee body through the hospital, and then sunshine, rain, and hail as John and I ate lunch at Marcos'. Like nature was acknowledging the wonder and beauty of life and its passing. I soooooo love that Little Guy. I am still so thankful that he came into our lives. I don't think I'd feel so, well, full, if I'd never had the chance to experience him. Amazing.

Did I tell you I woke up in the wee dark hours of almost-morning a month or so ago, and smelled the most beautiful scent of roses ever? It faded away and then came back again.

Life is amazing. That we are given gifts and situations that challenge and teach us, to help us grow, to help our love grow—that help us cherish every moment as purposeful and every thought as meaningful. This is a part of life and a part of who we are. I just hope the rest of our kiddos grow, live, and love for a very long time.

Love, Hannah

~~~

From: JohnandHannah@email.com
To: Krista@email.com
Sent: Friday, November 9, 2007
Subject: Update

Hello chum! How are you? Just wanted to let you know they'll be breaking my water on the 19th, around ten a.m. or so. My body's already progressing and the doctor says he's fine for me to go into labor now, at any time.

The house is clean, my bag is packed, the car seat is installed …. I think the real waiting has just begun! I'll keep you posted. The kids and I baked a cake today and tomorrow we will celebrate Clinton's first birthday. :-)

Love, Hannah

*****

GAVIN James Sullivan, a dear, little pipsqueak, weighing in at six pounds and four ounces, was born on November 19th, 2007. Almost an exact year from Clinton's birth, he fit our arms and filled our hearts perfectly.

In no time at all, this new life was an established member of the family circle.

"Here, Mikey." I gestured to the bed. "Sit down and you can have a turn holding him." Gavin was beginning to snuffle around in my arms, a precursor to wailing. I placed him carefully in Mikey's lap, where he instantly grew calm. Mikey leaned down and kissed the top of Gavin's round, fuzzy head, then looked up at me.

"Mama, Bavin said 'Ehhh!' 'cause he wann-ed a kiss. So I kissed him an' he stopped!"

*****

From: JohnandHannah@email.com
To: Krista@email.com
Sent: Friday, May 9, 2008
Subject: just realized …

I just realized something today. I know I've written before that I never know how to respond to the "how many children do you have" question, and that I just respond with as much info as I feel is right for the moment. Well, today I was chatting with one of the men on the track at the gym who has to be around eighty years old. He was talking about his children—how he had four living but had lost twins at birth.

That's when it struck me. I will never be "over" Clinton, like sometimes I feel people think I should be. He is my son, won't ever stop being my son .... We had him and raised him and loved him for his entire lifetime.

The man's comment, without even knowing my history, somehow validated my feelings. After all, he still mentions his twins, who must have been born at least fifty years ago. So, I'm fine with my Little Guy, and won't feel apologetic about any answer I give. I think about Clinton every day, especially while I'm nursing Gavin in the middle of the night. I feel so blessed to have had all of my little men and my one princess. I wish I could have bunches more ;-)

Thanks for listening!

Love, Hannah

~~~

From: JohnandHannah@email.com
To: Karen@email.com
Sent: Thursday, October 3, 2008
Subject: Thinking of you

Hey, Karen! I am so sorry about your dad. That must be hard to go through, but how awesome that you got to be there for him. You are so strong and amazing. YES, our thoughts are with you, along with bunches of hugs and loves.

Ellie's field-trip bus driver died last year, and we figured Clinton is getting a personal tour of heaven in that big yellow school bus. Now we picture everyone we know who dies, riding around on this bus with Clinton and the bus driver. And it makes us smile, picturing them all together. So, if you'd like your dad to get a ride, send him along. He can cuddle our Little Guy, and they can have grand adventures while waiting for us!

Please feel free to call or write if you need an ear or shoulder or heart—we'd be very happy to lend those parts!

Wishing you all the best and sending our love, Hannah and the gang

*****

"BUT, mom, what about the guy who did it? He died, too, didn't he?" On December 14th, 2012—*a day before Clinton's sixth death-day anniversary—a horrible tragedy had played out at a school in Newtown, Connecticut. Something I will never be able to understand. My daughter and I had decided those sweet children all had a spot on Clinton's school bus. And then she posed her question.*

"What about him, Sweetie?"

"Does he get to go on the bus, too?"

I thought about all the friends and family members we had placed on that bus over the years, and I knew my answer, but I wanted her to be able to come to her own conclusion. "Well, what do you think, Ellie? Do you think he should?" Waiting for her answer, I wondered how she'd balance her choice. It didn't take her long.

"I think he should be put on the bus."

A smile threatened to shimmer through the water in my eyes. "Yeah? And why is that?"

"Because he has a lot to learn about light and love, and Clinton can really help him with that."

All the Tomorrows to Come

The Secret of Life

Everyone has a story. Everyone. Sometimes we get so wrapped up in our own that we fail to recognize someone else's. Sometimes we forget to listen to all the words. And sometimes our happy ending is hiding in a sludge that appears to be anything but.

We let so many people flit through our lives without realizing the impact they potentially have on us, and we forget to watch for the traces we leave on others. Yet it's all there—written across our own souls, reflected in the eyes of our child, spread across the face of a stranger. Love. Love can leave the greatest impression of all.

Without Clinton, I wouldn't have found the joy of sharing someone's story, entering briefly into a life outside my own, and being able to offer love and support to someone I may know nothing about. The random eye-contact-with-a-smile, the friendly gesture or honest compliment made solely to give joy to someone else—those are beginning steps, the first pages.

But it's a whole new chapter, letting someone in. Being able to accept their kindness, their gift, their love. I had a hard time accepting anything from people; I thought it made me weak. Until it hit me. By accepting their gesture of love, I was actually giving them a gift. I was allowing them to feel needed and letting them have a chance to offer love into the world.

Without Clinton, I would not have witnessed how the longevity of a lifetime in no way reflects the significance of an individual life. In five short weeks, he accomplished more than most people do in five decades. He brought together strangers across the globe, united in hope and love; he taught people about grace and acceptance, about loving and letting go. He challenged some of the brightest medical minds, many at the beginning of their careers, when the impact would be the greatest. He created the opportunity for people to give of themselves and to grow in ways they never imagined.

Because of Clinton, I am more empathetic of other people and their stories. I know to slow down so I can take in the important things going on around me. I recognize the significance of reaching out to other people—to share that smile, that kindness—in order to lighten their load. I know that I can't always read someone's story in passing, but I know it's there. And I know I want to have a positive impact. I want the trace I leave to shine with hope and love. If I can make one person each day feel like they are important, worthy, respected, or cared for as a fellow human being, then I know it was a day well spent.

He changed me. And because of that, I can move through each day, hopefully bringing change to other people. And that change, that love, will keep growing, and spreading. Every day something good will happen, and somehow, some way, it can be traced back to the legacy of one small boy.

Clinton's Playlist
The Soundtrack of a Lifetime

1. *Don't Know Why* by Norah Jones
2. *Beautiful Boy (Darling Boy)* by John Lennon
3. *Backseat of a Greyhound Bus* by Sara Evans
4. *You're Beautiful* by James Blunt
5. *Niagara* by Sara Evans
6. *A Real Fine Place to Start* by Sara Evans
7. *Otis Redding* by Sara Evans
8. *If You're Going Through Hell* by Rodney Atkins
9. *Rockin' Horse* by Sara Evans
10. *Come Away with Me* by Norah Jones
11 *Feelin' the Same Way* by Norah Jones
12. *Cry* by James Blunt
13 *I've Got to See You Again* by Norah Jones
14. *Lone Star* by Norah Jones
15. *Painter Song* by Norah Jones
16. *My Heart Will Go On* by Celine Dion
17. *The Long Day Is Over* by Norah Jones
18. *Angel* by Sarah McLachlan
19. *Nightingale* by Norah Jones
20. *Somewhere Over the Rainbow* by Israel

Acknowledgements
Because Recognition is Important

FIRST AND FOREMOST, I offer my deepest, most sincere thanks to the staff of OHSU and Doernbecher Children's Hospital. You showed integrity, respect, strength, and love throughout every bit of our stay. You offered our son everything that he might live; you created an environment in which we could give Clinton the whole of ourselves.

Thank you to my husband John, who walks by my side, lives within my heart, and offers me the world.

Thank you to my children, Eleanor, Michael, Clinton, Gavin, Carter, and Olivia. You are the best parts of us, and you shine with a radiance that is all your own.

Thank you Krista, Karen, Amy, and Sarah for letting me share your words or the inspiration from your words. You are all strong, amazing, and loving women and I am so glad your lives have been a part of mine.

Thank you to my family and friends for your support throughout the entire process of Clinton's journey.

Thank you to Mom Betsy, the best mother-in-law ever, for walking through the memories with me and for making sure my facts were in line and my spelling was correct.

Thank you to my best writerly friends in the world, the women of the WorldWiseWriters group. Shoshona, Andrea, Jennelle, Jacky, and Rowanna—mothers, aunties, sisters, daughters, wives, friends, and writers extraordinaire. Your awesome eyeballs kept this tale in line. An extra special thanks to Ace, without whom the pages would never have made sense! Check out this amazing group of authors at http://www.worldwisewriters.com/

Thank you to some new wonderful friends, Paula and Veronica, early readers for "Five Weeks," and beautiful writers themselves.

Thank you to Patty Fewer, the best editor in the world. How did I get so lucky? Any remaining glitches are mine, and mine alone!

Thank you, Rebecca Sterling, for your fantastic cover work—a true reflection of what was in my heart. Visit her website at http://www.sterlingdesignstudios.com

And thank you, my lovely readers. You can help spread the light and love through your choices and actions, every day. Make every moment count.

YOU CAN HELP spread Clinton's story! Please post a review on
http://www.amazon.com/

About The Author

HANNAH SULLIVAN lives with her husband and children in Meridian, Idaho. A member of the WorldWideWriters group, she is the author of Thunder: The Shadows Are Stirring, a young adult fantasy-adventure novel. Favorite pastimes include eating chocolate and running.

Publishing Clinton's story has been a dream of Hannah's for many years. Everybody's story counts. If you have anything to share or ask, she would love to hear from you! Contact her at thunderstorybooks@gmail.com and visit her website at http://www.thunderstories.com

WorldWiseWriters

<u>For young adults:</u>
Crossfire **by Andrea Domanski**
Once a normal teenaged girl, now an Amazon warrior. Add in a bunch of kick-butt preternaturals and one maniacal demi-god and what have you got? The worst birthday ever!
Website: http://www.andreadomanski.com/
Also by **Andrea Domanski**: *Greco*; *Rogue*; and *Pandora*

Archer **by Jackie Gray**
Mmmm. Shoot an apple off his friend's head or lose his food, horse, and clothes? Some decisions require little thought.
Website: http://www.hengistarcher.co.uk
Also by **Jackie Gray**: *Rory*; *Reagan*; and *Slater*

Thunder: The Shadows Are Stirring **by Hannah Sullivan**
A rift between the layers of the world. A talking horse. Evil sliders. What's a girl to do when she's the only one who can save it all?
Website: http://www.thunderstories.com/

For adults:

The Faithful **by SM Freedman**

According to I Fidele, non-psychics are cockroaches. And the extermination is about to begin.

Website: http://www.smfreedman.com

Mirrored Time **by JD Faulkner**

New jobs aren't supposed to be this hard. Crazy half-gods, time travelers, and ex-gladiator thieves? Unemployment never looked so good.

Website: http://www.timearchivistsnovels.com

Death Wishes **by Rowanna Green**

When Jo Gold dies, all Hell lets loose in Heaven; she must live until her bucket list is fulfilled. Who better to help her than a rookie guardian angel? Think Coke Break guy with wings. Yummy!

Website: http://rockslikea.blogspot.co.uk

Also by **Rowanna Green**: *Triple Jeopardy*; *Fox Among Wolves*; and *Wolf in Sheep's Clothing*

******

If you'd like to view an excerpt from **Hannah Sullivan's** novel, *THUNDER: THE SHADOWS ARE STIRRING*, please continue reading.

The following is an excerpt of Hannah Sullivan's Young Adult Fantasy novel, ***THUNDER: THE SHADOWS ARE STIRRING***, available now at Amazon.com.

Thunder

Transition

(OLIVIA)

THE PRESSURE IN MY CHEST IS SO TIGHT, it's like someone's squeezing my lungs in their fists. I can't breathe. Realizing I need to do something to calm the frenzied racing of my heart, I try to adjust my position. But I can't move. And I definitely can't think of a way to release the pressure. If the squeezing doesn't stop, my vital organs will burst and Mom and Dad are going to freak that I've somehow managed to implode in the back seat of their car.

A surge of white light flares from behind my closed eyelids and the silence that follows is deep enough to make my eardrums thud. Steady and low and pulsating. The light fades to a dull red and then a recognizable sound penetrates my skull.

What on earth? Shouldn't I be hearing angel wings and harps? What, you may ask, am I getting instead?

Horses, apparently.

Seriously? I'm a city kid. I've never been around a real horse before, but I'm pretty sure I know my animal sounds. I swear I hear hoof beats and my body now seems to be moving to the same rhythm.

The heaviness in my chest releases and my body feels weightless and fractured, no longer connected to me. Then the sensation is gone and cold air is blasting against my back, shoving me forward into something firm and lumpy. It would help if I could move or at least open my eyes. Or *breathe*. I could probably make sense of whatever's happening. Instead, I let myself fall into nothingness and hope for the best.

Before

(OLIVIA)

"LIV!" MY DAD CALLS THROUGH THE HOUSE, "don't forget to grab that pile of snow stuff in the hallway. At the rate we're going, Gunther's cabin will be buried by the time we get there."

Rolling my eyes, I bounce down the stairs gripping my pillow as my backpack thumps against my spine, its heaviness wanting to tug me backward. We're having Thanksgiving at Dad's friend's house. Actually, to say "friend" doesn't cut it. Gunther is closer than a brother to my dad. We've all grown up on tales of how Dad was running as fast as he could into hoodlumdom (which I highly doubt is even a word, but who am I to question the sanctity of the stories?); and here comes Gunther Ryland, ten years older, ten shades darker, and about ten shoulders wider than pale, scrawny Dad.

Dad had been a smart kid. Really. Like skip-grades smart. But he never fit in and was often bored and looking for ways to express his inner hellion. Having no friends and ever-changing foster parents can lead to quirks like that. Gunther was a part of the Big Brothers Big Sisters program, and he started to join Dad both at school for lunch and out of school for "structured activities." Slowly he got Dad to refocus his "erstwhile energies into productive choices and long term goals."

Dad is now Dr. Joseph Williams, one of the area's top pediatricians at St. Helene's Hospital. While still in residency, he married Mom. Her name is Julia Malory and she's a Kindergarten teacher at Washington Elementary. They had yours truly and my two little brothers within a span of a few years. I, Olivia Grace, am thirteen and a half; Sam turned twelve back in July, and Jamie turned ten a week ago. My birthday's at the end of May.

We're taking a couple extra days off from school and driving to Gunther's amazingly spectacular home, six hours away and up in the mountains. He never married and has no kids of his own, but he does some fostering here and there for hard to place cases. Not that he'd ever call them that. Man, his brown eyes glint red if you even suggest one of his kids is a "case" or that they're trouble at all. He's got some magic touch turning them back into kids and getting them settled wherever they belong.

Now, this house of his …. Gunther calls it a cabin, but it is truly colossal, with exterior log walls and massive amounts of windows. Inside, there are two stone fireplaces and heated wood floors. The bedrooms have bunks, though the area rugs are plush enough you could sleep on those just the same. There's also a library, a game room, and a media room; the kitchen could be from a restaurant. Numerous patios and balconies overlook all the amazing views of the trees and distant lake.

At least, that's what I hear. I get dizzy going up three floors in an elevator, so I don't do much hanging over balconies or staring out of windows that show me how I could plunge to my death if the glass gave way.

You know, I've never known what Gunther does or if he has family around, but whenever we're with him I feel like we fit right into his carefully molded world. He's that easy to be with.

~~~

THREE HOURS INTO THE TRIP, frozen rain has begun to splat against the car windows. Dad's driving at the pace of a two-legged bug and the sky has become this non-color of whitish-gray. Snow will come next. The windshield wipers whir and scrape back and forth. I sigh and gaze over at Sam's video game, but I watch too long and feel my stomach begin to roll. Jamie's fallen asleep with his head lolling to the side, his drool teasing Sam's shoulder.

Car trips are not an area in my life where I shine. I close my eyes again and lower the volume of my iPod just enough to hear the rounded sounds and cadences of my parents' voices, but not enough to make out actual words. The SUV drones with a steady hum and I feel cocooned by the cushy seats and armor-like exterior.

When I wake up, my watch reads just after 4:30. It's awfully dark already. I pull out my ear buds and Jamie's wondering how much longer we have. I want to know the same thing, but I'm glad I wasn't the first one to ask, being the oldest and all.

"Sweets," Mom says, "we've got to go slow. We're in a white-out and Dad's doing what he can. We just have to sit tight till we make it over the pass. After that, we'll be able to make our turn-off."

Great. Because then come the switchbacks, the lack of any shoulder, and the sheer cliff drop down the right-hand side. Joy. If I didn't love Gunther so much, I'd seriously consider demanding to be left right here on the side of the road, snowstorm or not.

"This is taking forever," groans Jamie, shifting in his seat. "I can't even look out my window 'cause I can't see anything."

It *is* almost impossible to see anything, with the snow doing the whole "warp speed ahead" thing in our headlights. In the low beams, the trees could dub as a forest from Narnia. It's called a white-out for a reason. I'm pretty sure we should not be attempting to drive through it, but there's nowhere to pull over. Who knows if someone's behind us? Dad's turned off the radio and I can tell he's leaning forward, as if being five inches closer to the windshield is going to help him see better.

"What about a story?" Mom asks. About a million years ago, when I was almost three, she began to use car trips as a storytelling forum, to distract me from my impending hurl-fests. The stories should maybe seem dorky to us now that we're older, but they're not. We view them as a sport.

Mom calls them "Thunder Stories" and incorporates each of us kids into a Grand Adventure. We get to pick out a random animal or magical creature and she has to be able to fit them all into the storyline. Things can get kind of funny when she's trying to piece together a badger, an octopus, and a fairy's missing shadow. Somehow it always works out and the story flows like it's something she's read before.

They always begin the same: "Once upon a time there were three amazing children named Olivia, Samuel, and James. They all lived together at the tip-top of a beautiful mountain with their magical horse named Thunder, who loved them dearly and took care of them."

Thunder could run so fast he actually flew through the air, with the wind whipping across our backs as we held on tight; always Sam in the front, then Jamie, then me. I suppose I was the one responsible for keeping us from falling off Thunder's broad back. He had these magic saddle bags, like something from Harry Potter, which could hold any supplies we packed for our mission; Thunder would lead us to our destination and let us go. We were on our own, saving talking animals, magical creatures, ourselves, or the world in general.

Most often, the stories end in a celebration including lots of food. Mom loves food. She claims she runs almost any chance she gets, just so she can eat. I don't know if that's healthy or not, but I run with her so she can have the company. We've even done some local races together, so we've got this whole competitive thing going on. And even though Mom likes to claim it's about "bonding," I think it's just plain fun to have some time together. She doesn't have to get so psychological trying to explain it.

Anyway, this evening she tells a tale of a blinding snowstorm and the wondrous Thunder who soars through the sky carrying these three amazing children who must save an angel, a bat, and a Velociraptor from impending doom. Before we can get to the good stuff about the feast, our car gets hit from behind, hydroplanes across the road, and spins until it slams into a wall of rock. Where it crumples like a soda can.

****

Thank you for reading this excerpt. For more information about Hannah Sullivan's books and projects, please visit her website at http://www.thunderstories.com/

www.ingramcontent.com/pod-product-compliance
Lightning Source LLC
Chambersburg PA
CBHW021156020426

42331CB00003B/91